Better Homes and Gardens®

STIR-FRY
RECIPES

BETTER HOMES AND GARDENS® BOOKS
Editor: Gerald M. Knox
Art Director: Ernest Shelton
Managing Editor: David A. Kirchner

Food and Nutrition Editor: Nancy Byal
Department Head—Cook Books: Sharyl Heiken
Associate Department Heads: Sandra Granseth,
    Rosemary C. Hutchinson, Elizabeth Woolever
Senior Food Editors: Julia Malloy, Marcia Stanley,
    Joyce Trollope
Associate Food Editors: Barbara Atkins, Molly Culbertson,
    Linda Foley, Linda Henry, Lynn Hoppe, Jill Johnson,
    Mary Jo Plutt, Maureen Powers
Recipe Development Editor: Marion Viall
Test Kitchen Director: Sharon Stilwell
Test Kitchen Photo Studio Director: Janet Pittman
Test Kitchen Home Economists: Jean Brekke, Kay Cargill,
    Marilyn Cornelius, Maryellyn Krantz, Lynelle Munn,
    Dianna Nolin, Marge Steenson, Cynthia Volcko

Associate Art Directors: Linda Ford Vermie,
    Neoma Alt West, Randall Yontz
Copy and Production Editors: Marsha Jahns,
    Mary Helen Schiltz, Carl Voss, David A. Walsh
Assistant Art Directors: Faith Berven, Harijs Priekulis,
    Tom Wegner
Senior Graphic Designers: Alisann Dixon, Lynda Haupert,
    Lyne Neymeyer
Graphic Designers: Mike Burns, Mike Eagleton, Deb Miner,
    Stan Sams, Darla Whipple-Frain

Vice President, Editorial Director: Doris Eby
Executive Director, Editorial Services: Duane L. Gregg

Senior Vice President, General Manager: Fred Stines
Director of Publishing: Robert B. Nelson
Vice President, Retail Marketing: Jamie Martin
Vice President, Direct Marketing: Arthur Heydendael

STIR-FRY RECIPES
Editor: Lynn Hoppe
Copy and Production Editor: David A. Walsh
Graphic Designer: Faith Berven
Electronic Text Processor: Joyce Wasson
Contributing Photographers: Scott Little, Teri Sandison/Lightra
Food Stylists: Mable Hoffman, Janet Pittman
Contributing Illustrator: Tom Rosborough

On the front cover: *Szechuan Beef* (see recipe, page 16)

Our seal assures you that every recipe in *Stir-Fry Recipes*
has been tested in the Better Homes and Gardens® Test Kitchen.
This means that each recipe is practical and reliable, and
meets our high standards of taste appeal.

Stir-frying—easy, varied, and fun. It's easy! Even a beginner will find it a cinch to learn with our step-by-step photos and simple-to-follow directions.

For variety, sample recipes as diverse as Szechuan Beef, Sauerbraten-Style Stir-Fry, Lamb and Linguine, and Spicy-Hot Chicken and Zucchini.

And best of all, it's fun! You can take your stir-fry know-how one step further by creating original dishes. We've included a handy vegetable chart and "Create-a-Stir" recipes to help you. No matter what you're looking for, you'll find what you need and want in *Stir-Fry Recipes.*

GETTING STARTED

Far East cooks have perfected stir-frying over the centuries. Now you can put it to use in your kitchen. We'll tell you how to select and care for your equipment, how to prepare ingredients, and how to stir-fry like a pro. Take it from there and make a world of delicious stir-fry recipes.

What You'll Need

A long-handled spoon, a sharp knife, and a large, deep skillet—that's really all you need to stir-fry like a pro. But if you prefer equipment especially designed for stir-frying, a wok and some of the many available accessories may be for you.

Skillet

The wok in its elegant simplicity has advantages when it comes to stir-frying. Its bowl-shaped design offers more cooking surface and a more even distribution of heat without hot spots than a skillet does. And the wok's wide top makes it easy to stir and toss the foods without making a mess.

The choice—a wok or a skillet—is yours. If a wok is for you, the following hints will help you select and care for your wok.

Choosing a Wok

Although the basic bowl shape is common to all woks, you'll find a variety of sizes, styles, and materials. A 14- to 16-inch-diameter wok, the most common size, is perfect for household ranges and accommodates enough food for two to four servings.

The *classic wok* has a rounded bottom and needs a ring stand to stabilize it on the burner. A variation on the classic design that is especially well-suited for an electric range is the *flat-bottomed wok*. Because electric heat works best when it comes in contact with the pan, this design provides the advantage of resting directly on the heating unit.

Electric woks have the advantage of portability. Sometimes the food may take a little longer to cook as the electric wok's thermostat cycles heat on and off, but the food will still taste great.

After you decide on the style, you're ready to think about the material. Most woks are carbon steel, stainless steel, and aluminum. Carbon steel, the most common, has good heat-transfer qualities. You will need to thoroughly season your carbon steel wok initially and after each use. As your carbon steel wok becomes well seasoned with use, its color darkens.

Stainless steel, though it requires no seasoning, has poorer heat-transfer qualities than carbon steel. To improve this quality, many manufacturers wrap the exterior heating surface with aluminum or copper.

The third option, aluminum or aluminum alloy, has good heating properties and requires little care. Some aluminum woks darken with use, but an aluminum cleaner can remedy that.

The Ring Stand

Understanding the role of the ring stand in adjusting the wok's distance from the heat is important to your success in using the classic wok.

Classic Wok

For an electric range, turn up the wide side of the ring stand so the wok sits closer to the heating unit. For a gas range, elevating the wok actually places it over a hotter part of the gas flame. Place the ring stand over the largest burner with the narrow side up to attain this needed elevation.

Accessories

Indispensable in stir-frying is a long-handled utensil for keeping food in motion over high heat. A long-handled wooden spoon is a good choice. Or, you may choose a Chinese-style spatula, which has a wide, slightly curved, metal blade that is perfect for the job. For nonstick surfaces, choose wood or another material that will not damage the finish.

Another essential accessory is a sharp knife for cutting ingredients into bite-size pieces. An option to a knife is a wide-bladed cleaver, a utensil commonly used in the Orient. A cleaver, when handled correctly, is especially well-suited for efficient chopping of ingredients. It is handy, also, for gathering the ingredients to place in your wok.

Other accessories may be helpful when you stir-fry. Many woks come equipped with a long-handled ladle for serving and chopsticks for mixing, cooking, and eating. Some also include a bamboo brush, just the thing for cleaning your wok.

Caring for Your Wok
Like any cooking tool, your wok needs care to perform well. Just a few minutes of attention each time you use it will preserve the wok for many years of good cooking—regardless of the material it's made of.

A new carbon steel wok comes with a rust-resistant coating. To remove this coating, scrub the wok and lid thoroughly inside and out with cleanser or scouring pads and hot, soapy water. Rinse the wok thoroughly, then dry it with a towel. To be sure the wok is completely dry, heat it on

your range for a few minutes. To season a carbon steel wok, add 2 tablespoons of cooking oil to the wok; tilt and rotate the wok to coat with oil. Heat the oil over high heat till the wok and oil are very hot. Remove from heat. Allow the wok to cool, then use a paper towel to rub the oil in. If the lid is carbon steel, season it the same way. Just remove wooden handles and place the lid directly on the burner of your range.

To clean and reseason your carbon steel wok after each use, soak the wok in hot water (detergent is unnecesssary and unrecommended), then clean it well with a bamboo brush or loofah sponge. Rinse thoroughly and dry with a towel. Heat the wok on the range to ensure it is totally dry. Then add about a teaspoon of cooking oil to the wok and rub it in with a paper towel. Thoroughly clean and dry the wok's lid and rub it with oil if the lid is carbon steel.

Never put a seasoned wok into the dishwasher; the harsh detergents and hot water will destroy the seasoning you have worked to achieve. Also, using a dishwasher to clean a carbon steel wok may cause it to rust. Store your seasoned wok in a well-ventilated place. Long periods in a warm, airless cupboard can cause the oil used in seasoning to become rancid.

Aluminum and stainless steel woks require no seasoning and little care. Just use a stainless steel or aluminum cleaner as needed.

Some aluminum and stainless steel woks have

Flat-Bottomed Wok

interior nonstick coatings and need seasoning. Because the methods for seasoning and cleaning these woks depend on the type of coating, first check the manufacturer's directions. Most nonstick coatings need a thorough cleaning and drying, then a small amount of cooking oil rubbed over the interior surface. As with carbon steel woks, nonstick woks need open storage. Also, you should never scrub a nonstick wok with anything abrasive.

Electric woks deserve special consideration. Follow the care directions recommended for the interior surface material in your wok. If your wok is immersible for washing, be sure to remove any parts not immersible, such as the heat control. Thoroughly dry every part of the wok before you reassemble it or plug it in.

Cutting Terms

Slicing and bias slicing

To slice a food, make even cuts with a knife or cleaver into the food, perpendicular to the cutting surface. When a recipe calls for thin slices, make the cuts as close together as possible, about ⅛ to ¼ inch thick.

To bias-slice, hold the knife or cleaver at a 45-degree angle while you cut the food into slices, as pictured at right.

Bias slices cook more quickly because they have a greater exposed surface area than conventional slices have. Another plus for bias slicing: The shape adds visual interest to your dish.

Roll cutting

To roll-cut a food, hold a knife or cleaver at a 45-degree angle to the cutting surface to make the first cut, then give food a quarter- to half-turn before angle-cutting again. This cut makes distinctive shapes of cylindrical vegetables such as carrots.

Depending on the size of the vegetable, stir-fry timings for roll-cut vegetables can vary considerably. Generally, roll-cut slices need more cooking time than conventional slices or bias slices. Roll-cut carrots even need precooking.

Cutting julienne strips

To make julienne strips, cut the food with a sharp knife or cleaver into long, narrow strips resembling matchsticks. First, cut the food into slices about 2 inches long and ¼ to ½ inch thick. Stack the thin slices, then slice lengthwise again to make thin sticks.

In addition to their attractiveness, vegetables cut into julienne strips cook quickly because of their large exposed surface area.

Bias-slicing meat

Stir-frying does a wonderful job of cooking most kinds of meat. Part of the secret is the way you cut the meat before cooking begins. Slice it very thinly across the grain for optimum tenderness.

It's easiest to do this if you start by partially freezing the meat so it is firm, but not hard. After 45 to 60 minutes in the freezer, the meat should be firm enough to slice.

Hold a sharp knife or cleaver at a 45-degree angle to the cutting board while you thinly slice the meat. If the meat slices are large, cut them into bite-size pieces.

Stir-Fry Basics

Ready, set, stir-fry! To help you get started stir-frying up a storm, we have included the following step-by-step photographs.

As the name implies, stir-frying is a cooking method that involves stirring and frying a food simultaneously. The food is lifted and turned as it cooks quickly over high heat in just enough oil to prevent sticking.

Cooking food in a flash is the key to good stir-frying. It means that vegetables retain their crispness and color and meats come out tender, with the flavor and juices sealed inside.

To stir-fry foods quickly, food preparation is an important consideration. By cutting the food into small, thin pieces of uniform size, you increase the exposed cooking surface making quick cooking possible.

The quantity of food you stir-fry together is something to consider too. To cook quickly, these small pieces of food must come in contact with the surface of the hot wok. When too much food is in the wok at one time, the food really gets steamed rather than stir-fried. That's why we've geared most of our recipes to two to four main-dish servings. For a larger group, pull out a second wok and have a helper stir-fry alongside you.

You'll soon discover that stir-frying is a systematic way of cooking. For the greatest of ease, follow these seven basic steps: (1) Prepare all ingredients before starting to stir-fry. (2) Add the oil to the hot wok. (3) Stir-fry the seasonings in the hot oil. (4) Stir-fry the vegetables first and remove them from the wok or skillet. (5) Stir-fry the meat. (6) Cook sauce until it is thickened and bubbly. (7) Stir all the ingredients together.

Now follow along on this and the next three pages. Each step is detailed, using *Orange-Walnut Pork* (see recipe, page 26) as the example.

1 First, prepare all of the ingredients

It's important to have all of the ingredients ready to go before you start stir-frying, and for a very good reason. You'll find that once you start, the cooking goes too quickly for you to prepare ingredients as you go.

Go ahead and prepare everything—slice all of the ingredients, combine the sauce ingredients, precook any food that needs it, and start cooking the rice or pasta if the recipe calls for it.

Arrange all of the ingredients in dishes near the wok so you can reach them easily when you're ready to use them.

2 Add the cooking oil

Preheat a wok or large skillet over high heat. Start with the highest setting on your range. As you stir-fry, lower the heat if necessary to prevent scorching.

If using a wok, add 1 tablespoon of cooking oil in a ring around the upper part of the wok so it coats the sides as it runs to the center. If using a large skillet, add the oil; lift and tilt the skillet to coat the bottom with oil.

To test the hotness of the oil, add a single piece of vegetable to the hot wok. If it sizzles, proceed with cooking the vegetables and meat as directed in the recipe. Add more oil only as necessary to prevent sticking.

3 Stir-fry the seasoning in hot oil

By stir-frying minced garlic and grated gingerroot first, the ingredient's distinctive flavor seasons the oil used to cook all of the remaining ingredients.

Stir-fry the seasoning for 15 seconds. To stir-fry, just stir it into the hot oil, keeping the seasoning in constant motion. Remember that because the amount you will be stir-frying at one time is quite small, it is especially important to keep the seasoning moving the entire time so it doesn't burn over the high heat.

4 Stir-fry the vegetables
Now you are ready to stir-fry the slower-cooking vegetables, followed by those that cook more quickly. Use a spatula or long-handled spoon to gently lift and turn the pieces of food with a folding motion so it cooks evenly. Remember to keep the food moving at all times to prevent scorching. Remove vegetables after stir-frying.

Oops! Forgot to prepare an ingredient? Don't despair; just remove the wok or skillet from the heat and toss the food to cool it and slow down the cooking. Then transfer the food to a platter until you're ready to resume cooking.

5 Stir-fry the meat
After you've cooked the vegetables, stir-fry the meat, chicken, or fish. Since overloading the wok or skillet with food slows cooking, generally stir-fry no than ¾ pound of meat at a time.

This means that for most recipes, you'll begin by stir-frying only *half* of the meat until it is done, and removing it from the wok. Then you'll stir-fry the remaining *half* of the meat. Return all of the cooked meat to the wok or skillet.

If you need to add more cooking oil between the batches of meat, bring the oil to frying temperature before proceeding.

6 Cook the sauce until thickened and bubbly

To thicken the sauce, push the cooked meat from the center of the wok or skillet. Restir the sauce ingredients you've already combined; then pour the mixture into the center of the wok or skillet.

Cook the sauce, stirring constantly, till it thickens and bubbles over the entire surface. Cook and stir for any additional time as directed in the recipe. The extra time ensures that the thickener, usually cornstarch, is cooked. Uncooked thickener can cause a raw, starchy flavor.

7 Stir all of the ingredients together

The final step is to return all of the stir-fried ingredients to the wok. Stir everything together to coat with the sauce. Then cook and stir the mixture as directed in the recipe until heated through.

If you're adding an ingredient that needs gentle treatment, such as mandarin oranges or tomatoes, add it after you have returned the vegetables to the wok and stirred the mixture together. Instead of cooking and stirring, however, simply cover and cook as directed until heated through. Stir in nuts. To assure that your stir-fry is piping hot, serve immediately.

MAIN DISHES

Whether it's the mystique of the Orient or the variety of stir-fry cooking that lures you, discover what happens when East meets West.
These main dishes represent the best of both worlds. You'll find traditional dishes exalting the heritage of the Far East, stir-fried versions of Western favorites, and recipes that take something from each.

Beef

Beef and Brussels Sprouts

Szechuan peppercorns, also called flower peppercorns because of their shape, are fragrant and spicy, but milder than whole black pepper.

1 pound beef top round steak
3 tablespoons dry sherry
2 tablespoons cold water
2 tablespoons soy sauce
1½ teaspoons cornstarch
¾ teaspoon crushed whole
    black pepper *or* crushed
    Szechuan peppercorns
1 tablespoon cooking oil
1 clove garlic, minced
1 10-ounce package frozen
    brussels sprouts, thawed
    and cut in half
1 medium carrot, shredded
    (½ cup)
    Hot cooked bulgur wheat
    or rice

● Partially freeze beef; cut on the bias into thin bite-size strips. For sauce, stir together sherry, water, soy sauce, cornstarch, and pepper. Set aside.

● Preheat a wok or large skillet over high heat; add cooking oil. (Add more oil as necessary during cooking.) Stir-fry garlic in hot oil for 15 seconds. Add brussels sprouts; stir-fry for 2 minutes. Add carrot; stir-fry about 1 minute or till vegetables are crisp-tender. Remove vegetables from the wok.

● Add *half* of the beef to the hot wok or skillet. Stir-fry for 2 to 3 minutes or till done. Remove beef. Stir-fry remaining beef for 2 to 3 minutes or till done. Return all beef to the wok. Push beef from center of the wok.

● Stir sauce; add to center of the wok or skillet. Cook and stir till thickened and bubbly. Cook and stir for 30 seconds more. Return vegetables to the wok or skillet; stir ingredients together to coat with sauce. Cook and stir for 1 minute. Serve immediately over hot cooked bulgur wheat or rice. Makes 4 servings.

Burgundy Beef

Shredded carrot adds color to this stir-fried version of the popular entrée.

1 pound beef top round steak
⅓ cup cold water
⅓ cup burgundy
1 tablespoon cornstarch
1 teaspoon instant beef
    bouillon granules
1 teaspoon catsup
¼ teaspoon dried thyme,
    crushed
1 tablespoon cooking oil
4 ounces fresh mushrooms,
    sliced (1½ cups)
1 medium carrot, shredded
    (½ cup)
2 green onions, sliced
    (¼ cup)
    Hot cooked noodles

● Partially freeze beef; cut on the bias into thin bite-size strips. For sauce, stir together water, burgundy, cornstarch, bouillon granules, catsup, and thyme. Set aside.

● Preheat a wok or large skillet over high heat; add cooking oil. (Add more oil as necessary during cooking.) Stir-fry mushrooms, carrot, and onions in hot oil about 1½ minutes or till crisp-tender. Remove vegetables from the wok.

● Add *half* of the beef to the hot wok or skillet. Stir-fry for 2 to 3 minutes or till done. Remove beef. Stir-fry remaining beef for 2 to 3 minutes. Return all beef to the wok or skillet. Push beef from center of the wok.

● Stir sauce; add to center of the wok or skillet. Cook and stir till thickened and bubbly. Cook and stir for 2 minutes more. Return vegetables to the wok or skillet; stir ingredients together to coat with sauce. Cook and stir for 1 minute. Serve immediately atop noodles. Makes 4 servings.

Szechuan Beef

Like most Szechuan dishes, our version of Szechuan Beef is peppery hot and richly seasoned. If you like, serve it with hot cooked rice or noodles to help cut the hotness.

1 pound beef top round steak
5 carrots, roll cut (1½ cups)
2 tablespoons dry sherry
1 tablespoon soy sauce
1 tablespoon hot bean sauce
¾ to 1 teaspoon crushed
    Szechuan peppercorns
1 tablespoon cooking oil
1 teaspoon chili oil*
2 cups fresh pea pods *or*
    one 6-ounce package
    frozen pea pods, thawed
1 15-ounce can straw
    mushrooms, drained
½ cup peanuts
    Garlic chives or small
    green onions (optional)

● Partially freeze beef; cut on the bias into thin bite-size strips. Cook carrots, covered, in a small amount of boiling salted water for 3½ minutes; drain. For sauce, stir together dry sherry, soy sauce, hot bean sauce, and crushed Szechuan peppercorns. Set sauce aside.

● Preheat a wok or large skillet over high heat; add cooking oil and chili oil. (Add more cooking oil as necessary during cooking.) Stir-fry carrots in hot oil for 30 seconds. Add pea pods; stir-fry for 1 minute. Add straw mushrooms; stir-fry about 1 minute more or till vegetables are crisp-tender. Remove the vegetables from the wok.

● Add *half* of the beef to the hot wok or skillet. Stir-fry for 2 to 3 minutes or till done. Remove beef. Stir-fry remaining beef for 2 to 3 minutes. Return all beef to the wok or skillet. Push beef from center of the wok.

● Add sauce to center of the wok or skillet. Cook and stir about 30 seconds or till heated through. Return vegetables; stir ingredients together to coat with sauce. Cook and stir for 1 minute. Stir in peanuts. Garnish with garlic chives or green onions, if desired. Serve immediately. Makes 4 servings.

*Chili oil is a spicy, red-colored oil seasoned by chili peppers. You will find it in an oriental market.

Zesty Beef and Cabbage

Pepperoni and an apple-juice-and-mustard sauce give this robust, stir-fried main dish its zing.

1 pound beef top round steak
½ cup apple juice *or* cider
4 teaspoons Dijon-style
    mustard
2 teaspoons cornstarch
1 tablespoon cooking oil
½ of a small head cabbage,
    shredded (4 cups)
½ of a 4-ounce package sliced
    pepperoni, coarsely
    chopped

● Partially freeze beef; cut on the bias into thin bite-size strips. For sauce, stir together apple juice or cider, mustard, and cornstarch. Set aside.

● Preheat a wok or large skillet over high heat; add cooking oil. (Add more oil as necessary during cooking.) Stir-fry cabbage in hot oil about 3 minutes or till crisp-tender. Remove cabbage from the wok.

● Add *half* of the beef to the hot wok or skillet. Stir-fry for 2 to 3 minutes or till done. Remove beef. Stir-fry remaining beef for 2 to 3 minutes. Return all beef to the wok or skillet. Push from center of the wok.

● Stir sauce; add to center of the wok or skillet. Cook and stir till thickened and bubbly. Cook and stir for 1 minute more. Return cabbage to the wok or skillet; add pepperoni. Stir ingredients together to coat with sauce. Cover and cook for 1 minute. Serve immediately. Makes 4 servings.

Szechuan Beef

Gingered Beef and Cauliflower

The skin of gingerroot wrinkles with age. Look for a tuber with a smooth outer skin.

1 pound beef top round steak
½ cup cold water
3 tablespoons soy sauce
1 tablespoon cornstarch
1 tablespoon cooking oil
2 tablespoons grated
    gingerroot
½ of a medium head
    cauliflower, sliced
    (2 cups)
    Hot cooked rice *or* warm
    chow mein noodles
2 tablespoons snipped chives
    (optional)

● Partially freeze beef; cut on the bias into thin bite-size strips. For sauce, stir together water, soy sauce, and cornstarch. Set sauce aside.

● Preheat a wok or large skillet over high heat; add oil. (Add more oil as necessary during cooking.) Stir-fry gingerroot in hot oil for 15 seconds. Add cauliflower; stir-fry about 5 minutes or till crisp-tender. Remove cauliflower.

● Add *half* of the beef to the hot wok or skillet. Stir-fry for 2 to 3 minutes or till done. Remove beef. Stir-fry remaining beef for 2 to 3 minutes or till done. Return all beef to the wok or skillet. Push from center of the wok.

● Stir sauce; add to center of the wok or skillet. Cook and stir till thickened and bubbly. Cook and stir for 1 minute more. Return cauliflower to the wok or skillet; stir ingredients together to coat with sauce. Cook and stir for 1 minute. Serve immediately over hot cooked rice or warm chow mein noodles. Sprinkle with snipped chives, if desired. Makes 4 servings.

Fruity Beef Stir-Fry

When served in the Almond-Rice Crust, this saucy beef-and-fruit stir-fry resembles a pie. Unlike most pies, however, you'll need to serve it with a spoon.

1 pound beef top round steak
1 8-ounce can pineapple
    chunks
⅓ cup cold water
2 tablespoons soy sauce
1 tablespoon cornstarch
    Almond-Rice Crust
1 tablespoon cooking oil
1 teaspoon grated gingerroot
1 medium apple, coarsely
    chopped (1 cup)
1 11-ounce can mandarin
    orange sections, drained

● Partially freeze beef; cut on the bias into thin bite-size strips. Drain pineapple, reserving juice. If necessary, add enough water to juice to make ⅓ cup liquid. For sauce, stir together reserved pineapple liquid, the ⅓ cup water, soy sauce, and cornstarch. Set aside. Prepare and bake the Almond-Rice Crust.

● While the crust is baking, preheat a wok or large skillet over high heat; add cooking oil. (Add more oil as necessary during cooking.) Stir-fry gingerroot in hot oil for 15 seconds. Add *half* of the beef; stir-fry for 2 to 3 minutes or till done. Remove beef. Stir-fry remaining beef for 2 to 3 minutes. Return all beef. Push from center of the wok.

● Stir sauce; add to center of the wok. Cook and stir till thickened and bubbly. Cook and stir for 2 minutes more. Add pineapple and apple; stir ingredients together. Cover and cook for 2 minutes. Gently stir in mandarin oranges. Cover and cook for 1 minute. Turn into baked crust. Serve at once. Makes 4 servings.

Almond-Rice Crust: Stir together 1 beaten *egg*, 1 cup *cold cooked rice* (cooked in unsalted water), ⅔ cup chopped toasted *almonds*, and 1 tablespoon *soy sauce*. Press into a greased 10-inch pie plate, pressing rice mixture against sides to form a crust. Cover with foil. Bake crust in a 325° oven for 10 minutes.

Peppery Beef

Bean threads, also called cellophane noodles, add oriental flair. (Pictured on page 31.)

1 pound beef top round steak
2 green onions, sliced (¼ cup)
¼ cup soy sauce
1 tablespoon sugar
2 tablespoons cooking oil
2 cloves garlic, minced
½ teaspoon pepper
¼ teaspoon ground red pepper
6 dried mushrooms
¼ cup snipped lily buds
1 tablespoon cornstarch
1 ounce bean threads
   (optional)
½ pound fresh broccoli,
   cut up (2 cups) (see tip,
   page 67)
1 medium zucchini, cut into
   2-inch-long julienne strips
2 small sweet red, yellow,
   and/or green peppers, cut
   into ¾-inch pieces (¾ cup)

● Partially freeze beef; cut on the bias into thin bite-size strips. For marinade, combine onions, soy, sugar, *1 tablespoon* of the oil, garlic, pepper, and red pepper. Add beef, stirring to coat. Cover and marinate at room temperature for 30 minutes or in the refrigerator for 2 hours, stirring occasionally.

● Meanwhile, rehydrate mushrooms and lily buds (see below); slice mushrooms. Stir together cornstarch and ⅓ cup *cold water*. If using bean threads, break into 4-inch lengths; cook in boiling water about 5 minutes or till tender. Drain; keep warm.

● Preheat a wok over high heat; add remaining 1 tablespoon oil. (Add more oil as necessary.) Stir-fry broccoli in hot oil for 1 minute. Add zucchini; stir-fry for 30 seconds. Add pepper pieces; stir-fry about 1½ minutes or till crisp-tender. Remove.

● Add *half* of the beef mixture to the hot wok. Stir-fry for 2 to 3 minutes or till done. Remove. Stir-fry remaining beef mixture for 2 to 3 minutes. Return all beef mixture. Push from center.

● Stir cornstarch mixture; add to center of the wok. Cook and stir till bubbly. Cook and stir for 1 minute more. Return vegetables; add mushrooms and lily buds. Stir ingredients together to coat with sauce. Cook and stir for 1 minute. Serve at once with bean threads, if desired. Makes 4 servings.

Rehydrating dried mushrooms and lily buds
Soak mushrooms and lily buds in enough warm water to cover about 30 minutes or till rehydrated. Squeeze to drain thoroughly. Thinly slice mushrooms, discarding the stems.

Beef Stir-Fry with Mushrooms

Soy sauce, red wine, and molasses make a robust sauce.

1 pound beef top round steak
⅓ cup cold water
¼ cup soy sauce
2 tablespoons dry red wine
4 teaspoons cornstarch
1 tablespoon molasses *or* honey
1 tablespoon cooking oil
8 ounces fresh mushrooms, sliced (3 cups)
5 green onions, bias-sliced into 1-inch lengths (1 cup)
Hot cooked rice

● Partially freeze beef; cut on the bias into thin bite-size strips. For marinade, in a medium mixing bowl stir together water, soy sauce, wine, cornstarch, and molasses. Add beef, stirring to coat well. Cover and marinate at room temperature for 30 minutes or in the refrigerator for 2 hours, stirring occasionally. Drain well, reserving marinade. Set aside.

● Preheat a wok or large skillet over high heat; add oil. (Add more oil as necessary during cooking.) Stir-fry mushrooms and green onions in hot oil about 2 minutes or till crisp-tender. Remove vegetables from the wok.

● Add *half* of the beef to the hot wok or skillet. Stir-fry for 2 to 3 minutes or till done. Remove beef. Stir-fry remaining beef for 2 to 3 minutes. Return all beef to the wok. Push from center of the wok or skillet.

● Stir marinade; add to center of the wok or skillet. Cook and stir till thickened and bubbly. Cook and stir for 1 minute more. Return vegetables to the wok or skillet; stir ingredients together to coat with sauce. Cook and stir for 1 minute. Serve immediately over hot cooked rice. Makes 4 servings.

Beer-Sauced Beef

Bacon and beer add gusto to this hearty stir-fry with a Bavarian influence.

1 pound beef top round steak
1 12-ounce can (1½ cups) beer
2 tablespoons cornstarch
2 teaspoons brown sugar
1½ teaspoons instant beef bouillon granules
¾ teaspoon dried thyme, crushed
⅛ teaspoon pepper
4 slices bacon, cut into ½-inch pieces
1 tablespoon cooking oil
½ of a medium head cauliflower, broken into flowerets (2 cups)
2 cups broccoli flowerets
Hot cooked spaetzle *or* noodles
2 tablespoons snipped parsley

● Partially freeze beef; cut on the bias into thin bite-size strips. For sauce, stir together beer, cornstarch, brown sugar, bouillon granules, thyme, and pepper. Set aside.

● In a wok or large skillet cook bacon pieces over medium heat till crisp. Remove bacon; drain and set aside. Discard bacon drippings. Add cooking oil to the wok or skillet. (Add more oil as necessary during cooking.) Stir-fry cauliflower in hot oil over high heat for 2 minutes. Add broccoli; stir-fry about 3 minutes or till vegetables are crisp-tender. Remove vegetables from the wok or skillet.

● Add *half* of the beef to the hot wok or skillet. Stir-fry for 2 to 3 minutes or till done. Remove beef. Stir-fry remaining beef for 2 to 3 minutes. Remove beef.

● Stir sauce; add to the wok or skillet. Cook and stir till thickened and bubbly. Cook and stir for 2 minutes more. Return vegetables and beef to the wok or skillet; stir ingredients together to coat with sauce. Cook and stir for 1 minute. Serve immediately over hot cooked spaetzle or noodles. Top with bacon and parsley. Makes 4 servings.

Sauerbraten-Style Stir-Fry

Traditional sauerbraten recipes require 36 to 72 hours of marinating; our stir-fried version using bite-size pieces of beef needs only 30 minutes to marinate.

1 pound beef top round steak
½ cup water
½ cup red wine vinegar
1 teaspoon sugar
½ teaspoon salt
2 whole black peppercorns, crushed
Dash ground ginger
½ of a medium onion, sliced
3 lemon slices
4 whole cloves
1 bay leaf
¼ cup crushed gingersnaps
1 tablespoon cooking oil
2 medium carrots, thinly bias sliced (1 cup)
2 stalks celery, thinly bias sliced (1 cup)
Hot cooked noodles *or* spaetzle

● Partially freeze beef; cut on the bias into thin bite-size strips. For marinade, stir together water, red wine vinegar, sugar, salt, crushed peppercorns, and ginger. Stir in onion, lemon slices, cloves, and bay leaf. Add beef, stirring to coat well. Cover and marinate at room temperature for 30 minutes or in the refrigerator for 2 hours, stirring occasionally. Remove and discard lemon slices, cloves, and bay leaf. Drain beef and onion, reserving marinade. Stir gingersnaps into reserved marinade. Set aside.

● Preheat a wok or large skillet over high heat; add cooking oil. (Add more oil as necessary during cooking.) Stir-fry carrots in hot oil for 2 minutes. Add celery; stir-fry about 3 minutes or till vegetables are crisp-tender. Remove the vegetables from the wok or skillet.

● Add *half* of the beef and onion mixture to the hot wok or skillet. Stir-fry about 3 minutes or till done. Remove mixture. Stir-fry remaining beef and onion mixture about 3 minutes. Return all beef to the wok. Push from center of the wok.

● Stir marinade mixture; add to center of the wok or skillet. Cook and stir till thickened and bubbly. Return vegetables to the wok or skillet; stir ingredients together to coat with sauce. Cook and stir for 1 minute. Serve immediately over hot cooked noodles or spaetzle. Makes 4 servings.

When Time Is A Problem

With just a little planning ahead, you can have your stir-fried meal on the table in minutes. Up to 24 hours before mealtime, prepare meat, vegetables, and sauce as directed in the recipe.

Refrigerate ingredients in separate, airtight containers until needed. You'll find that a few minutes of advance preparation can eliminate the time crunch later on.

South-of-the-Border
Stir-Fry

South-of-the-Border Stir-Fry

For unusual and fun dining, this spicy stir-fry goes atop tortilla chips.

1 pound beef top round steak
1 cup chili salsa
¼ cup cold water
2 tablespoons snipped parsley
2 teaspoons vinegar
¾ teaspoon cornstarch
½ teaspoon sugar
½ teaspoon ground cumin
¼ teaspoon pepper
⅛ teaspoon ground cinnamon
1 tablespoon cooking oil
1 clove garlic, minced
1 small onion, chopped
1 7-ounce can whole kernel
   corn with sweet peppers
8 ounces tortilla chips
   (5 cups)
1 cup shredded lettuce
   (optional)
½ cup shredded Monterey
   Jack cheese *or* Monterey
   Jack cheese with jalapeño
   peppers (2 ounces)
   (optional)
   Hot chili peppers
   (optional)

● Partially freeze beef; cut on the bias into thin bite-size strips. For sauce, in a small bowl stir together *half* of the chili salsa, water, parsley, vinegar, cornstarch, sugar, cumin, pepper, cinnamon, and ¼ teaspoon *salt*. Set aside.

● Preheat a wok or large skillet over high heat; add cooking oil. (Add more oil as necessary during cooking.) Stir-fry garlic in hot oil for 15 seconds. Add onion; stir-fry about 2 minutes or till tender. Remove onion.

● Add *half* of the beef to the hot wok. Stir-fry for 2 to 3 minutes or till done. Remove beef. Stir-fry remaining beef for 2 to 3 minutes or till done. Return all beef to the wok or skillet. Push beef from center of the wok.

● Stir sauce; add to center of the wok or skillet. Cook and stir till thickened and bubbly. Cook and stir for 2 minutes more. Return onion to the wok or skillet; add corn. Stir ingredients together to coat with sauce. Cover and cook for 1 minute. Arrange the tortilla chips on 4 individual dinner plates. Top with meat mixture; remaining chili salsa; lettuce, if desired; and cheese, if desired. Garnish with hot chili peppers, if desired. Serve immediately. Makes 4 servings.

No-Chop Beef Stir-Fry

Eliminate the chopping and you have eliminated the most time-consuming part of stir-frying.

⅓ cup cold water
3 tablespoons soy sauce
2 tablespoons dry sherry
2 teaspoons cornstarch
¼ teaspoon ground ginger
1 tablespoon cooking oil
3 cups loose pack frozen
   mixed oriental vegetables,
   thawed
1 pound lean ground beef
   Hot cooked rice *or* warm
   chow mein noodles

● For sauce, stir together water, soy sauce, sherry, cornstarch, and ginger. Set aside.

● Preheat a wok or large skillet over high heat; add cooking oil. (Add more oil as necessary during cooking.) Stir-fry vegetables in hot oil about 3 minutes or till crisp-tender. Remove vegetables from the wok.

● Crumble *half* of the ground beef into the hot wok or skillet. Stir-fry about 3 minutes or till done. Remove beef; drain off fat. Stir-fry remaining beef about 3 minutes. Drain off fat. Return all beef to the wok. Push from center of the wok.

● Stir sauce; add to center of the wok or skillet. Cook and stir till bubbly. Cook and stir for 2 minutes more. Return vegetables; stir ingredients together. Cook and stir for 1 minute. Serve at once over rice or chow mein noodles. Makes 4 servings.

Pork

Five Spice Pork

Five spice powder is a pleasing blend of star anise, cinnamon, cloves, fennel, and pepper.

1 pound boneless pork
⅓ cup dry sherry
3 tablespoons teriyaki sauce
1 clove garlic, minced
½ teaspoon five spice powder
Water
2 teaspoons cornstarch
1 tablespoon cooking oil
4 ounces jicama, peeled and cut into ¾-inch cubes (1 cup), *or* one 8-ounce can whole water chestnuts, drained and quartered
½ pound fresh broccoli, cut up (2 cups) (see tip, page 67)
½ cup peanuts

● Partially freeze pork; cut on the bias into thin bite-size strips. For marinade, stir together sherry, teriyaki sauce, garlic, and five spice powder. Add pork, stirring to coat well. Cover and marinate at room temperature for 30 minutes or in the refrigerator for 2 hours, stirring occasionally. Drain pork, reserving marinade. Add enough water to reserved marinade to make ⅔ cup. Stir into cornstarch. Set aside.

● Preheat a wok or large skillet over high heat; add oil. (Add more oil as necessary.) If using jicama, stir-fry in hot oil for 1 minute (if using water chestnuts, set aside). Add broccoli; stir-fry about 3 minutes or till crisp-tender. Remove vegetables.

● Add *half* of the pork to the hot wok or skillet. Stir-fry about 3 minutes or till no longer pink. Remove pork. Stir-fry remaining pork about 3 minutes. Return all pork to the wok. If using water chestnuts, stir into meat. Push mixture from center of the wok.

● Stir marinade mixture; add to center of the wok. Cook and stir till thickened and bubbly. Cook and stir for 30 seconds more. Return vegetables; stir ingredients together. Cook and stir for 1 minute. Stir in peanuts. Serve immediately. Makes 4 servings.

Pineapple-Mustard Pork

Sweet red pepper, if available, adds a vibrant splash of color to this dish with a tropical flair.

1 pound boneless pork
1 8¼-ounce can pineapple chunks
2 tablespoons Dijon-style mustard
2 teaspoons cornstarch
½ teaspoon instant chicken bouillon granules
1 tablespoon cooking oil
5 green onions, bias-sliced into 1-inch lengths (1 cup)
1 medium sweet red *or* green pepper, cut into ¾-inch pieces (¾ cup)

● Partially freeze pork; cut on the bias into thin bite-size strips. Drain pineapple, reserving juice. For sauce, stir together the reserved pineapple juice, mustard, cornstarch, and chicken bouillon granules. Set aside.

● Preheat a wok or large skillet over high heat; add cooking oil. (Add more oil as necessary during cooking.) Stir-fry green onions and the pepper pieces in hot oil about 1½ minutes or till vegetables are crisp-tender. Remove vegetables from the wok.

● Add *half* of the pork to the hot wok. Stir-fry pork about 3 minutes or till no longer pink. Remove pork. Stir-fry remaining pork about 3 minutes. Return all pork to the wok. Push pork from the center of the wok.

● Stir sauce; add to center of the wok. Cook and stir till thickened and bubbly. Cook and stir for 30 seconds more. Return vegetables; stir ingredients together. Stir in pineapple. Cover and cook for 1 minute. Serve immediately. Makes 4 servings.

Fried Brown Rice with Pork

Chilling the cooked rice before adding it to the stir-fry prevents it from absorbing more liquid and becoming gummy.

½ pound boneless pork
2 tablespoons dry sherry
2 tablespoons soy sauce
⅛ teaspoon pepper
1 tablespoon cooking oil
2 beaten eggs
1 tablespoon cooking oil
1 clove garlic, minced
1 medium onion, chopped
   (½ cup)
2 cups chilled, cooked brown
   rice
1 cup frozen peas, thawed

● Partially freeze the pork; cut on the bias into thin bite-size strips. For sauce, stir together dry sherry, soy sauce, and pepper. Set aside.

● Preheat a wok or large skillet over medium heat; add 1 tablespoon oil. Add eggs; lift and tilt the wok or skillet to form a thin layer of egg. Cook, without stirring, for 2 to 3 minutes or till just set (see below). Remove from heat; use a spatula to cut into bite-size strips. Remove the cooked egg strips from the wok.

● Return the wok to heat. Add 1 tablespoon oil to the hot wok or skillet. (Add more oil as necessary during cooking.) Stir-fry garlic in hot oil over high heat for 15 seconds. Add onion; stir-fry about 2 minutes or till tender. Remove onion from the wok.

● Add all the pork to the hot wok. Stir-fry about 3 minutes or till no longer pink. Stir sauce, brown rice, and peas into pork. Cook and stir for 1 minute. Stir in egg strips and onion. Cover and cook for 1 minute. Serve immediately. Makes 4 servings.

Cooking the eggs
Preheat a wok or large skillet over medium heat; add 1 tablespoon cooking oil. Pour eggs into the hot wok. Lift and tilt the wok or skillet to form a thin layer of egg on the bottom and partially up the sides of the wok. Cook, without stirring, for 2 to 3 minutes or till just set. Remove the wok or skillet from the heat; use a spatula to cut into bite-size strips. Remove the egg strips from the wok or skillet.

Sweet-and-Sour Pork with Nectarines

Sliced nectarines add a new twist to an old-time favorite. (Pictured on the back cover.)

1 pound boneless pork
1 cup peach *or* apricot nectar
⅓ cup honey
⅓ cup red wine vinegar
2 tablespoons cornstarch
1 tablespoon soy sauce
1 tablespoon cooking oil
1 medium carrot, thinly bias sliced (½ cup)
1 stalk celery, thinly bias sliced (½ cup)
1 medium green pepper, cut into ½-inch pieces (¾ cup)
4 medium nectarines, sliced (2 cups)
  Hot cooked rice

● Partially freeze pork; cut on the bias into thin bite-size strips. For sauce, stir together peach or apricot nectar, honey, vinegar, cornstarch, and soy sauce. Set aside.

● Preheat a wok or large skillet over high heat; add cooking oil. (Add more oil as necessary during cooking.) Stir-fry carrot in hot oil for 1 minute. Add celery; stir-fry for 1½ minutes. Add green pepper; stir-fry about 1½ minutes or till vegetables are crisp-tender. Remove vegetables from the wok.

● Add *half* of the pork to the hot wok or skillet. Stir-fry about 3 minutes or till pork is no longer pink. Remove pork. Stir-fry remaining pork about 3 minutes. Return all pork to the wok or skillet. Push from center of the wok.

● Stir sauce; add to center of the wok. Cook and stir till thickened and bubbly. Cook and stir for 2 minutes more. Return vegetables to the wok or skillet; stir ingredients together to coat with sauce. Gently stir in nectarines. Cover and cook for 2 minutes. Serve immediately over hot cooked rice. Makes 4 servings.

Orange-Walnut Pork

Although four cloves of garlic may seem a lot, this stir-fry has a pleasantly mild flavor. (Pictured on pages 10–13.)

1 pound pork tenderloin
½ pound green beans, bias-sliced into 1-inch pieces
1 teaspoon finely shredded orange peel
½ cup orange juice
2 tablespoons dry sherry
1½ teaspoons cornstarch
1½ teaspoons instant chicken bouillon granules
1 tablespoon cooking oil
4 cloves garlic, minced
2 medium carrots, thinly bias sliced (1 cup)
5 green onions, bias-sliced into 1-inch lengths (1 cup)
1 medium green pepper, cut into thin strips (1 cup)
1 11-ounce can mandarin orange sections, drained
½ cup walnut halves
  Hot cooked rice

● Partially freeze the pork; cut on the bias into thin slices. Cook green beans, covered, in a small amount of boiling salted water for 4 minutes; drain. For sauce, stir together orange peel, orange juice, sherry, cornstarch, and bouillon granules. Set aside.

● Preheat a wok or large skillet over high heat; add cooking oil. (Add more oil as necessary during cooking.) Stir-fry garlic in hot oil for 15 seconds. Add carrots; stir-fry for 1 minute. Add green beans; stir-fry for 1½ minutes. Add green onions and green pepper; stir-fry about 1½ minutes or till vegetables are crisp-tender. Remove vegetables from the wok.

● Add *half* of the pork to the hot wok or skillet. Stir-fry about 3 minutes or till no longer pink. Remove pork. Stir-fry remaining pork about 3 minutes or till no longer pink. Return all pork to the wok. Push from center of the wok.

● Stir sauce; add to center of the wok or skillet. Cook and stir till thickened and bubbly. Cook and stir for 1 minute more. Return vegetables to the wok or skillet; stir ingredients together to coat with sauce. Add mandarin orange sections. Cover and cook for 1 minute. Gently stir in walnuts. Serve immediately over hot cooked rice. Makes 4 servings.

Gingered Pork
(see recipe, page 29)

Spicy Pork with Baby Corn

Baby sweet corn is so tender you can eat the cob, too.

1 pound boneless pork
½ cup cold water
1 tablespoon bean sauce
1 teaspoon cornstarch
¼ teaspoon ground red pepper
1 tablespoon cooking oil
3 stalks celery, thinly bias
   sliced (1½ cups)
1 7-ounce jar whole baby
   sweet corn, drained and
   cut in half crosswise
8 cherry tomatoes, halved
   Hot cooked rice

● Partially freeze pork; cut on the bias into thin bite-size strips. For sauce, stir together water, bean sauce, cornstarch, and red pepper. Set aside.

● Preheat a wok or large skillet over high heat; add cooking oil. (Add more oil as necessary during cooking.) Stir-fry celery in hot oil about 3 minutes or till crisp-tender. Remove celery from the wok or skillet.

● Add *half* of the pork to the hot wok or skillet. Stir-fry about 3 minutes or till no longer pink. Remove pork. Stir-fry remaining pork about 3 minutes or till no longer pink. Return all pork to the wok or skillet. Stir in corn. Push mixture from center of the wok or skillet.

● Stir sauce; add to center of the wok. Cook and stir till thickened and bubbly. Cook and stir for 1 minute more. Return celery to the wok or skillet; stir ingredients together to coat with sauce. Arrange tomatoes atop. Cover and cook for 1 minute. Serve immediately over rice. Makes 4 servings.

Marinated Pork Stir-Fry

A savory wine marinade seasons this attractive combination of pork and vegetables.

1 pound boneless pork
⅓ cup burgundy
1 tablespoon Worcestershire
   sauce
½ teaspoon dried thyme,
   crushed
¼ teaspoon celery salt
¼ teaspoon dried oregano,
   crushed
¼ teaspoon dried sage,
   crushed
⅛ teaspoon pepper
   Several dashes bottled hot
   pepper sauce
¼ cold water
2 teaspoons cornstarch
1 tablespoon cooking oil
1 medium zucchini, halved
   lengthwise and sliced
   ¼ inch thick (1¼ cups)
1 medium green pepper, cut
   into thin strips (1 cup)
6 cherry tomatoes, halved

● Partially freeze pork; cut pork on the bias into thin bite-size strips. For marinade, stir together burgundy, Worcestershire sauce, thyme, celery salt, oregano, sage, pepper, and hot pepper sauce. Add pork, stirring to coat well. Cover and marinate at room temperature for 30 minutes or in the refrigerator for 2 hours, stirring occasionally. Drain pork, reserving ¼ cup marinade. Stir cold water and cornstarch into the reserved marinade. Set aside.

● Preheat a wok or large skillet over high heat; add cooking oil. (Add more oil as necessary during cooking.) Stir-fry zucchini in hot oil for 1½ minutes. Add green pepper; stir-fry about 1½ minutes or till vegetables are crisp-tender. Remove vegetables from the wok or skillet.

● Add *half* of the pork to the hot wok. Stir-fry about 3 minutes or till no longer pink. Remove pork. Stir-fry remaining pork about 3 minutes or till no longer pink. Return all pork to the wok. Push pork from center of the wok.

● Stir marinade mixture; add to center of the wok. Cook and stir till thickened and bubbly. Cook and stir for 1 minute more. Return vegetables to the wok; stir ingredients together to coat with marinade mixture. Arrange tomatoes atop. Cover and cook for 1 minute. Serve immediately. Makes 4 servings.

Gingered Pork

The dark green leaves of bok choy provide a rich color contrast to the other ingredients. (Pictured on page 27.)

1 pound boneless pork
⅓ cup oyster sauce
¼ cup dry sherry
2 tablespoons water
1 teaspoon sugar
¾ cup cold water
4 teaspoons cornstarch
1 tablespoon cooking oil
1 tablespoon grated
   gingerroot
2 medium carrots, cut into
   julienne strips (⅔ cup)
4 cups sliced bok choy
½ of an 8-ounce can (½ cup)
   sliced water chestnuts,
   drained
   Hot cooked rice

● Partially freeze pork; cut on the bias into thin bite-size strips. For marinade, stir together oyster sauce, sherry, the 2 tablespoons water, and sugar. Add pork, stirring to coat well. Cover and marinate at room temperature for 30 minutes or in the refrigerator for 2 hours, stirring occasionally. Drain pork, reserving marinade. Stir the ¾ cup cold water and cornstarch into reserved marinade. Set aside.

● Preheat a wok or large skillet over high heat; add cooking oil. (Add more oil as necessary during cooking.) Stir-fry gingerroot in hot oil for 15 seconds. Add carrots; stir-fry for 1 minute. Add bok choy; stir-fry about 3 minutes or till vegetables are crisp-tender. Remove from the wok.

● Add *half* of the pork to the hot wok. Stir-fry about 3 minutes or till no longer pink. Remove pork. Stir-fry remaining pork about 3 minutes. Return all pork to the wok. Stir in water chestnuts. Push from center of the wok.

● Stir marinade mixture; add to center of the wok. Cook and stir till thickened and bubbly. Cook and stir for 1 minute more. Return vegetables; stir ingredients together. Cook and stir for 1 minute. Serve immediately over rice. Makes 4 servings.

Slicing bok choy

For a distinct oriental touch and a sweet, mild flavor, add bok choy to your stir-fried dishes. To prepare bok choy, pull off one celerylike stalk, then thinly slice the white stem and dark green leaves into bite-size pieces. Repeat with additional stalks as needed.

Stir-Frying Outdoors

Combine a love of the outdoors and a love of stir-fry. Just take your wok or skillet outside! Your stir-fries will be just as tasty, and it's a fun break from routine.

Grill It!

First, make sure your wok or skillet fits the grill. For a wok, place the ring stand and wok on the grate. Place a skillet directly on the grate. The bottom of the utensil should be about 6 inches from where the coals will be. Also, make sure you have some ventilation space between the utensil and the grill's edge. Remove the utensil and the grate. Cover wooden parts of the utensil with several layers of foil to protect them from the heat.

Light the coals. The coals are hot enough when you can comfortably hold your hand 6 inches above the coals for no more than two seconds. Spread out the hot coals in a single layer; return your utensil and grate. Now, stir-fry and enjoy!

Or Campfire Cook It!

To stir-fry without a grill, arrange three or four rocks about the same size to act as a stand. Cover any wooden parts of your wok or skillet with several layers of foil. Balance the utensil on the rocks, keeping its bottom about 6 inches from where the charcoal or wood will be. Remove the utensil. Arrange the charcoal or wood inside rocks. Light the fire and test the hotness as directed at left. Return the utensil to its resting place on the rocks, and proceed stir-frying.

Woks Made for Grills
Some barbecue grills, like the one below, have woks especially made to fit them. These woks may be as large as 24 inches in diameter. They rest on the grill at the correct distance from the hot coals and allow for ventilation between the wok and the grill. Check with your grill's manufacturer to see if woks are available.

Lamb

Lamb with Hoisin Sauce

Hoisin sauce is sometimes referred to as the Chinese catsup. In a pinch—and in small amounts—you can substitute a mixture of one part catsup and one part molasses.

1	pound boneless lamb
3	medium carrots, roll cut (1 cup)
⅔	cup cold water
2	tablespoons hoisin sauce
2	tablespoons soy sauce
1	tablespoon dry sherry
2	teaspoons cornstarch
1	tablespoon cooking oil
½	pound fresh broccoli, cut up (2 cups) (see tip, page 67)
1	8-ounce can sliced water chestnuts, drained
	Hot cooked bulgur wheat

● Partially freeze the lamb; cut on the bias into thin bite-size strips. Cook carrots, covered, in a small amount of boiling salted water for 3½ minutes; drain. For sauce, stir together ⅔ cup cold water, hoisin sauce, soy sauce, dry sherry, and cornstarch. Set sauce aside.

● Preheat a wok or large skillet over high heat; add cooking oil. (Add more oil as necessary during cooking.) Stir-fry carrots and broccoli in hot oil about 3 minutes or till vegetables are crisp-tender. Remove vegetables from the wok.

● Add *half* of the lamb to the hot wok or skillet. Stir-fry about 3 minutes or till done. Remove lamb. Stir-fry remaining lamb about 3 minutes or till done. Return all lamb to the wok or skillet. Stir in water chestnuts. Push mixture from center of the wok or skillet.

● Stir sauce; add to center of the wok or skillet. Cook and stir till thickened and bubbly. Cook and stir for 1 minute more. Return vegetables to the wok or skillet; stir ingredients together to coat with sauce. Cook and stir for 1 minute. Serve immediately over hot cooked bulgur wheat. Makes 4 servings.

Lamb with Wine Sauce

Dijon-style mustard adds pizzazz to the palate-pleasing sauce.

1	pound boneless lamb
¼	cup cold water
¼	cup dry white wine
1	tablespoon Dijon-style mustard
2	teaspoons cornstarch
1	teaspoon instant chicken bouillon granules
1	tablespoon cooking oil
5	green onions, bias-sliced into 1-inch lengths (1 cup)
½	cup thinly sliced fresh mushrooms
¼	cup sliced almonds
	Hot cooked fine noodles

● Partially freeze lamb; cut on the bias into thin bite-size strips. For sauce, stir together water, wine, mustard, cornstarch, and bouillon granules. Set aside.

● Preheat a wok or large skillet over high heat; add cooking oil. (Add more oil as necessary during cooking.) Stir-fry green onions and mushrooms in hot oil about 1½ minutes or till onions are crisp-tender. Remove vegetables from the wok.

● Add *half* of the lamb to the hot wok. Stir-fry about 3 minutes or till done. Remove lamb. Stir-fry remaining lamb about 3 minutes. Return all lamb. Push from center of the wok.

● Stir sauce; add to center of the wok or skillet. Cook and stir till thickened and bubbly. Cook and stir for 1 minute more. Return vegetables to the wok or skillet; stir ingredients together to coat with sauce. Cook and stir for 1 minute. Stir in almonds. Serve immediately over noodles. Makes 4 servings.

Lamb Bundles

Use your fingers to dip these lamb-filled lettuce packages into the tart Lemon-Apricot Sauce.

1 pound boneless lamb
2 tablespoons cold water
2 tablespoons dry sherry
2 tablespoons soy sauce
2 teaspoons cornstarch
 Lemon-Apricot Sauce
1 tablespoon cooking oil
1 teaspoon grated gingerroot
¼ cup chopped almonds
¼ cup fresh bean sprouts
2 green onions, thinly
 sliced (¼ cup)
16 small romaine *or* Bibb
 lettuce leaves

● Partially freeze lamb; cut on the bias into thin bite-size strips. For sauce, stir together water, sherry, soy sauce, and cornstarch. Set aside. Prepare Lemon-Apricot Sauce; keep warm.

● Meanwhile, preheat a wok or large skillet over high heat; add cooking oil. (Add more oil as necessary during cooking.) Stir-fry gingerroot in hot oil for 15 seconds. Add almonds, bean sprouts, and green onions; stir-fry about 1½ minutes or till onions are crisp-tender. Remove vegetables and nuts from the wok.

● Add *half* of the lamb to the hot wok. Stir-fry about 3 minutes or till done. Remove lamb. Stir-fry remaining lamb about 3 minutes. Return all lamb to the wok. Push from center.

● Stir sauce; add to center of the wok. Cook and stir till bubbly. Cook and stir for 1 minute more. Return vegetables and nuts; stir ingredients together. Cook and stir for 1 minute. Fill lettuce leaves with lamb mixture (see below). Serve immediately. Pass Lemon-Apricot Sauce for dipping. Makes 4 servings.

Lemon-Apricot Sauce: In a small saucepan combine ⅔ cup *apricot preserves,* 2 tablespoons *lemon juice,* 1 tablespoon *hoisin sauce,* and ½ teaspoon grated *gingerroot.* Cook over low heat till heated through, stirring occasionally.

Assembling Lamb Bundles
To assemble bundles, spoon one rounded tablespoon of lamb mixture onto the center of each lettuce leaf. Fold up the leaf from the bottom to the center. Fold two sides of the leaf over the filling so the edges of the leaf overlap about 1 inch. Place, folded side of the bundle down, on a serving platter.

Lamb and Linguine

Before cooking the linguine, break it in half. The shorter pieces will distribute more evenly among the other stir-fry ingredients.

1 pound boneless lamb
½ cup teriyaki sauce
3 ounces linguine
½ of an 8-ounce can (½ cup) tomato sauce
1 tablespoon dry sherry
2 teaspoons cornstarch
1 tablespoon cooking oil
1 medium zucchini, sliced ¼ inch thick (1¼ cups)
2 stalks celery, thinly bias sliced (1 cup)
1 small onion, thinly sliced
1 medium green pepper, cut into thin strips (1 cup)

● Partially freeze lamb; cut on the bias into thin bite-size strips. Add lamb to teriyaki sauce, stirring to coat well. Cover and marinate at room temperature for 30 minutes or in the refrigerator for 2 hours, stirring occasionally. Meanwhile, cook the linguine in boiling *unsalted* water according to package directions; drain. Keep warm.

● Drain lamb, reserving ¼ cup teriyaki sauce. For sauce, stir together reserved teriyaki sauce, tomato sauce, sherry, and cornstarch. Set aside.

● Preheat a wok or large skillet over high heat; add cooking oil. (Add more oil as necessary during cooking.) Stir-fry zucchini, celery, and onion in hot oil for 1½ minutes. Add green pepper; stir-fry about 1½ minutes or till vegetables are crisp-tender. Remove vegetables from the wok.

● Add *half* of the lamb to the hot wok. Stir-fry about 3 minutes or till done. Remove lamb. Stir-fry remaining lamb about 3 minutes. Return all lamb to the wok. Push from center.

● Stir sauce; add to center of the wok. Cook and stir till thickened and bubbly. Cook and stir for 1 minute more. Return vegetables; add linguine. Stir ingredients together. Cook and stir for 1 minute. Serve immediately. Makes 4 servings.

Gyro-Style Pockets

The traditional Greek gyro (pronounced JEE-row or YEE-row) sandwich is made from highly seasoned, pressed meat grilled on a vertical rotisserie.

¾ pound boneless lamb
1 medium cucumber
½ of an 8-ounce carton (½ cup) plain yogurt
2 teaspoons all-purpose flour
¾ teaspoon instant chicken bouillon granules
½ teaspoon dried oregano, crushed
¼ teaspoon garlic powder Dash dried thyme, crushed
1 tablespoon cooking oil
1 medium onion, chopped
2 large pita bread rounds, halved
4 romaine *or* leaf lettuce leaves

● Partially freeze lamb; cut on the bias into thin bite-size strips. Halve cucumber lengthwise; trim off ends and scoop out seeds. Cut cucumber into ¼-inch slices. For sauce, stir together yogurt, flour, bouillon granules, oregano, garlic powder, thyme, and ⅛ teaspoon *pepper*. Set aside.

● Preheat a wok or large skillet over high heat; add oil. (Add more oil as necessary during cooking.) Stir-fry cucumber in hot oil for 2 minutes. Add onion; stir-fry about 2 minutes or till cucumber is crisp-tender. Remove vegetables.

● Stir-fry all the lamb about 3 minutes or till done. Push lamb from center. Reduce heat. Add sauce to center of the wok. Cook and stir till thickened and bubbly. Return vegetables to the wok or skillet; stir ingredients together to coat with sauce. Cook and stir for 1 minute.

● Line pita halves with lettuce leaves. Spoon lamb mixture into pita halves. Top with thinly sliced onion rings, if desired. Serve immediately. Makes 4 servings.

Poultry

Chicken Aloha

Canned pie filling and vinegar provide plenty of sweet-and-sour flavor—the easy way!

2 whole medium chicken breasts (1½ pounds total), skinned and boned
1 21-ounce can pineapple *or* apple pie filling
3 tablespoons vinegar
3 tablespoons soy sauce
1 teaspoon instant chicken bouillon granules
1 tablespoon cooking oil
2 medium carrots, thinly bias sliced (1 cup)
2 cups fresh pea pods *or* one 6-ounce package frozen pea pods, thawed
Warm chow mein noodles

● Cut chicken into 1-inch pieces. For sauce, stir together pie filling, vinegar, soy sauce, bouillon granules, and 2 tablespoons *water*. Set aside.

● Preheat a wok or large skillet over high heat; add cooking oil. (Add more oil as necessary during cooking.) Stir-fry carrots in hot oil for 3 minutes. Add pea pods; stir-fry about 2 minutes or till vegetables are crisp-tender. Remove vegetables from the wok or skillet.

● Add *half* of the chicken to the hot wok or skillet. Stir-fry about 3 minutes or till done. Remove the chicken. Stir-fry the remaining chicken about 3 minutes or till done. Return all the chicken to the wok or skillet.

● Stir sauce into chicken. Return vegetables to the wok or skillet; stir ingredients together to coat with sauce. Cook and stir for 1 minute. Serve immediately over warm chow mein noodles. Makes 4 servings.

Spicy-Hot Chicken and Zucchini

You may wish to add your own toppers, such as shredded cheddar cheese or sour cream.

2 whole medium chicken breasts (1½ pounds total), skinned and boned
⅔ cup hot-style tomato juice
1 to 2 tablespoons chopped, drained canned jalapeño peppers
2 teaspoons cornstarch
½ teaspoon instant chicken bouillon granules
1 tablespoon cooking oil
1 medium zucchini, bias-sliced ¼ inch thick
2 stalks celery, thinly bias sliced (1 cup)
1 small onion, chopped
1 medium tomato, cut into thin wedges
8 ounces tortilla chips

● Cut chicken into thin bite-size strips. For sauce, stir together tomato juice, jalapeño peppers, cornstarch, and bouillon granules. Set aside.

● Preheat a wok or large skillet over high heat; add cooking oil. (Add more oil as necessary during cooking.) Stir-fry zucchini and celery in hot oil for 1 minute. Add onion; stir-fry about 2 minutes or till vegetables are crisp-tender. Remove vegetables from the wok or skillet.

● Add *half* of the chicken to the hot wok or skillet. Stir-fry for 2 to 3 minutes or till done. Remove chicken. Stir-fry remaining chicken for 2 to 3 minutes. Return all chicken to the wok. Push chicken from center of the wok.

● Stir sauce; add to center of the wok or skillet. Cook and stir till thickened and bubbly. Cook and stir for 1 minute more. Return vegetables to the wok; stir ingredients together to coat with sauce. Arrange tomatoes atop. Cover and cook for 1 minute. Arrange tortilla chips on 4 individual dinner plates. Top with the chicken mixture. Serve immediately. Makes 4 servings.

Papaya Chicken

Papaya Chicken

If papaya is unavailable at your grocery store, substitute another fruit such as nectarines, pears, plums, or oranges.

1 whole medium chicken
  breast (¾ pound total),
  skinned and boned
⅓ cup water
2 tablespoons dry white wine
2 tablespoons soy sauce
1½ teaspoons cornstarch
1 tablespoon cooking oil
1 stalk celery, thinly
  bias-sliced into ½-inch
  lengths (½ cup)
½ of a papaya, seeded,
  peeled, and cut into bite-
  size pieces (1 cup)
¼ cup macadamia nuts *or*
  whole blanched almonds
  Hot cooked rice
  Papaya slices (optional)

● Cut chicken into 1-inch pieces. For marinade, stir together water, dry white wine, and soy sauce. Add chicken, stirring to coat well. Cover and marinate at room temperature for 30 minutes or in the refrigerator for 2 hours, stirring occasionally. Drain the chicken, reserving the marinade. Combine cornstarch and the reserved marinade. Set aside.

● Preheat a wok or large skillet over high heat; add cooking oil. (Add more oil as necessary during cooking.) Stir-fry celery in hot oil for 3 to 4 minutes or till crisp-tender. Remove celery from the wok or skillet.

● Add all the chicken to the hot wok or skillet. Stir-fry about 3 minutes or till done. Push chicken from center of the wok.

● Stir marinade mixture; add to center of the wok. Cook and stir till thickened and bubbly. Cook and stir for 30 seconds more. Return celery; add papaya. Stir ingredients together to coat with sauce. Cover and cook for 1 minute. Stir in nuts. Serve immediately over hot cooked rice. Garnish with papaya slices, if desired. Makes 2 servings.

Herbed Chicken and Vegetables

Our taste panel members agreed that marjoram and thyme make a delectable combo in this attractive and elegant entrée.

2 whole medium chicken
  breasts (1½ pounds total),
  skinned and boned
½ pound green beans, bias-
  sliced into 1-inch pieces
¼ cup chicken broth
3 tablespoons dry white wine
1½ teaspoons cornstarch
½ teaspoon sugar
¼ teaspoon dried marjoram,
  crushed
¼ teaspoon dried thyme,
  crushed
1 tablespoon cooking oil
1 medium zucchini *or* yellow
  summer squash, thinly
  bias sliced (1¼ cups)
5 green onions, bias-sliced
  into 1-inch lengths (1 cup)
½ cup cashews

● Cut chicken into 1-inch pieces. Cook beans, covered, in a small amount of boiling salted water for 4 minutes; drain. For sauce, stir together chicken broth, wine, cornstarch, sugar, marjoram, and thyme. Set aside.

● Preheat a wok or large skillet over high heat; add cooking oil. (Add more oil as necessary during cooking.) Stir-fry green beans and zucchini or yellow summer squash in hot oil for 1½ minutes. Add green onions; stir-fry about 1½ minutes or till vegetables are crisp-tender. Remove vegetables from the wok.

● Add *half* of the chicken to the hot wok or skillet. Stir-fry about 3 minutes or till done. Remove chicken. Stir-fry remaining chicken about 3 minutes. Return all chicken to the wok. Push chicken from center of the wok.

● Stir sauce; add to center of the wok or skillet. Cook and stir till thickened and bubbly. Cook and stir for 1 minute more. Return vegetables to the wok or skillet; stir ingredients together to coat with sauce. Cook and stir for 1 minute. Stir in cashews. Serve immediately. Makes 4 servings.

Chicken with Oranges

For variety, serve this colorful dish atop a mixture of equal parts of wild rice and long grain rice.

2 whole medium chicken
   breasts (1½ pounds total),
   skinned and boned
3 medium carrots, roll cut
¼ cup dry sherry
2 tablespoons cold water
2 tablespoons soy sauce
1 tablespoon brown sugar
1½ teaspoons cornstarch
   Few drops bottled hot
   pepper sauce
1 tablespoon cooking oil
1 clove garlic, minced
5 green onions, bias-sliced
   into 1-inch lengths (1 cup)
1 11-ounce can mandarin
   orange sections, drained
¾ cup walnut halves
   Hot cooked rice

● Cut chicken into 1-inch pieces. Cook carrots, covered, in a small amount of boiling salted water for 3½ minutes; drain. For sauce, stir together sherry, the 2 tablespoons water, soy sauce, brown sugar, cornstarch, and hot pepper sauce. Set aside.

● Preheat a wok or large skillet over high heat; add cooking oil. (Add more oil as necessary during cooking.) Stir-fry garlic in hot oil for 15 seconds. Add carrots; stir-fry for 1 minute. Add green onions; stir-fry about 1½ minutes or till vegetables are crisp-tender. Remove vegetables from the wok.

● Add *half* of the chicken to the hot wok or skillet. Stir-fry about 3 minutes or till done. Remove chicken. Stir-fry remaining chicken about 3 minutes or till done. Return all chicken to the wok. Push chicken from center of the wok.

● Stir sauce; add to center of the wok or skillet. Cook and stir till thickened and bubbly. Cook and stir for 1 minute more. Return vegetables to the wok or skillet; stir ingredients together to coat with sauce. Add orange sections. Cover and cook for 1 minute. Stir in walnuts. Serve immediately over hot cooked rice. Makes 4 servings.

Chicken with Asparagus

To quickly thaw frozen asparagus, place unwrapped asparagus in a colander. Then run warm water over the asparagus for about 1 minute.

2 whole medium chicken
   breasts (1½ pounds total),
   skinned and boned
½ cup cold water
¼ cup dry white wine
3 tablespoons soy sauce
1 tablespoon cornstarch
1 tablespoon honey
1 teaspoon instant chicken
   bouillon granules
1 tablespoon cooking oil
2 teaspoons grated gingerroot
1 10-ounce package frozen
   cut asparagus, thawed
5 green onions, bias-sliced
   into 1-inch lengths (1 cup)
½ cup sliced fresh mushrooms
1 8-ounce can water chestnuts, drained and halved
   Hot cooked rice

● Cut chicken into thin bite-size strips. For sauce, stir together water, wine, soy sauce, cornstarch, honey, and bouillon granules. Set aside.

● Preheat a wok or large skillet over high heat; add cooking oil. (Add more oil as necessary during cooking.) Stir-fry gingerroot in hot oil for 15 seconds. Add asparagus; stir-fry for 1½ minutes. Add green onions and mushrooms; stir-fry about 1½ minutes or till vegetables are crisp-tender. Remove vegetables from the wok or skillet.

● Add *half* of the chicken to the hot wok or skillet. Stir-fry for 2 to 3 minutes or till done. Remove chicken. Stir-fry remaining chicken for 2 to 3 minutes or till done. Return all chicken to the wok or skillet. Stir in water chestnuts. Push chicken mixture from center of the wok.

● Stir sauce; add to center of the wok. Cook and stir till thickened and bubbly. Cook and stir for 2 minutes more. Return vegetables to the wok or skillet; stir ingredients together to coat with sauce. Cook and stir for 1 minute. Serve immediately over rice. Makes 4 servings.

You'll get about ¾ pound of meat from two whole medium chicken breasts (1½ pounds total).

1 To bone a whole chicken breast, place the breast, bone side down, on a cutting board. Cut through the meat to the bone near the center back of the whole chicken breast. Then proceed with cutting the meat from the bone as shown below.

2 Starting from the breastbone, cut the meat away from one side of the breast, using a sawing motion. Press the flat side of the knife blade against the rib bones. As you cut, gently pull meat up and away from the bones. Repeat for the other side.

Curried Chicken

Curry powder is a ground blend of 16 or more different spices. Although the blend varies widely, it almost always includes cumin, coriander, fenugreek, turmeric, and red pepper.

2 whole medium chicken
   breasts (1½ pounds total),
   skinned and boned
1 tablespoon cornstarch
1 tablespoon curry powder
1 teaspoon instant chicken
   bouillon granules
½ teaspoon dried thyme,
   crushed
1 tablespoon cooking oil
1 clove garlic, minced
3 stalks celery, thinly
   bias sliced (1½ cups)
1 medium onion, cut into thin
   wedges
8 cherry tomatoes, halved
½ cup peanuts
½ cup raisins
   Hot cooked couscous *or* rice
   Condiments* (optional)

● Cut chicken into 1-inch pieces. For sauce, stir together cornstarch, curry powder, bouillon granules, thyme, and 1¼ cups *cold water*. Set aside.

● Preheat a wok or large skillet over high heat; add cooking oil. (Add more oil as necessary during cooking.) Stir-fry garlic in hot oil for 15 seconds. Add celery and onion; stir-fry about 3 minutes or till celery is crisp-tender. Remove vegetables from the wok or skillet.

● Add *half* of the chicken to the hot wok or skillet. Stir-fry about 3 minutes or till done. Remove chicken. Stir-fry remaining chicken about 3 minutes. Return all chicken to the wok. Push chicken from center of the wok.

● Stir sauce; add to center of the wok. Cook and stir till thickened and bubbly. Cook and stir for 2 minutes more. Return vegetables to the wok or skillet; stir ingredients together to coat with sauce. Add tomatoes. Cover and cook for 1 minute. Stir peanuts and raisins into the chicken mixture. Serve immediately atop hot cooked couscous or rice. If desired, pass condiments. Makes 4 servings.

*Crumbled, cooked bacon; toasted coconut; chutney; and/or sliced bananas.

Chicken with Oyster Sauce

Oyster sauce, available in most grocery stores, is a thickened sauce of oyster juices and salt. It is lighter in color and thicker than soy sauce, but just as salty.

2 whole medium chicken
   breasts (1½ pounds total),
   skinned and boned
3 tablespoons oyster sauce
2 tablespoons cold water
2 tablespoons dry sherry
2 teaspoons cornstarch
1 tablespoon cooking oil
1 medium carrot, thinly
   bias sliced (½ cup)
6 cups sliced bok choy
1 stalk celery, bias-sliced into
   ½-inch lengths (½ cup)
5 green onions, bias-sliced
   into 1-inch lengths (1 cup)
   Hot cooked rice

● Cut chicken into 1-inch pieces. For sauce, stir together oyster sauce, water, sherry, and cornstarch. Set aside.

● Preheat a wok or large skillet over high heat; add cooking oil. (Add more oil as necessary during cooking.) Stir-fry carrot in hot oil for 1 minute. Add bok choy and celery; stir-fry for 2½ minutes. Add green onions; stir-fry about 1½ minutes or till vegetables are crisp-tender. Remove vegetables from the wok.

● Add *half* of the chicken to the hot wok or skillet. Stir-fry about 3 minutes or till done. Remove chicken. Stir-fry remaining chicken about 3 minutes or till done. Return all chicken to the wok. Push chicken from center of the wok.

● Stir sauce; add to center of the wok. Cook and stir till thickened and bubbly. Cook and stir for 1 minute more. Return vegetables; stir ingredients together to coat with sauce. Cook and stir for 1 minute. Serve immediately over hot cooked rice. Makes 4 servings.

Curried Chicken

Tarragon Chicken

Tarragon and lemon juice in the wine sauce make this main dish light and freshly seasoned.

2 whole medium chicken
    breasts (1½ pounds total),
    skinned and boned
½ cup cold water
½ cup dry white wine
4 teaspoons cornstarch
1½ teaspoons instant chicken
    bouillon granules
1 teaspoon dried tarragon,
    crushed
1 teaspoon lemon juice
1 tablespoon cooking oil
½ pound fresh broccoli,
    cut up (2 cups) (see tip,
    page 67)
5 green onions, bias-sliced
    into 1-inch lengths (1 cup)
1 medium sweet red *or* green
    pepper, cut into ¾-inch
    pieces (¾ cup)

● Cut chicken into 1-inch pieces. For sauce, stir together water, wine, cornstarch, bouillon granules, tarragon, and lemon juice. Set aside.

● Preheat a wok or large skillet over high heat; add cooking oil. (Add more oil as necessary during cooking.) Stir-fry broccoli in hot oil for 1½ minutes. Add green onions and pepper pieces; stir-fry about 1½ minutes or till vegetables are crisp-tender. Remove vegetables from the wok.

● Add *half* of the chicken to the hot wok or skillet. Stir-fry about 3 minutes or till done. Remove chicken. Stir-fry remaining chicken about 3 minutes. Return all chicken to the wok. Push from center of the wok.

● Stir sauce; add to center of the wok or skillet. Cook and stir till thickened and bubbly. Cook and stir for 2 minutes more. Return vegetables to the wok or skillet; stir ingredients together to coat with sauce. Cook and stir for 1 minute. Serve immediately. Makes 4 servings.

Sweet-and-Sour Chicken Livers

The combination of chopped apple and apple juice is a refreshing addition to this sweet-and-sour-sauced stir-fry.

½ cup apple juice
3 tablespoons brown sugar
2 tablespoons red wine
    vinegar
2 teaspoons cornstarch
1½ teaspoons soy sauce
1 tablespoon cooking oil
1 clove garlic, minced
2 medium carrots, thinly
    bias sliced (1 cup)
5 green onions, bias-sliced
    into 1-inch lengths (1 cup)
1 medium green pepper, cut
    into ¾-inch pieces (¾ cup)
½ pound chicken livers,
    halved
1 medium apple, coarsely
    chopped (1 cup)
    Hot cooked rice

● For sauce, stir together apple juice, brown sugar, vinegar, cornstarch, and soy sauce. Set aside.

● Preheat a wok or large skillet over high heat; add cooking oil. (Add more oil as necessary during cooking.) Stir-fry garlic in hot oil for 15 seconds. Add carrots; stir-fry for 2½ minutes. Add green onions and green pepper; stir-fry about 1½ minutes or till vegetables are crisp-tender. Remove the vegetables from the wok or skillet.

● Add all the chicken livers to the hot wok or skillet. Stir-fry for 3 to 4 minutes or till just pink. Push chicken livers from center of the wok or skillet.

● Stir sauce; add to center of the wok or skillet. Cook and stir till thickened and bubbly. Cook and stir for 1 minute more. Return vegetables to the wok or skillet; stir ingredients together to coat with sauce. Stir in apple. Cover and cook for 1 minute. Serve immediately over hot cooked rice. Makes 4 servings.

Lemon-Marinated Chicken

For even more lemon flavor, stir ½ teaspoon finely shredded lemon peel into the marinade.

2 whole medium chicken
    breasts (1½ pounds total),
    skinned and boned
⅓ cup water
¼ cup lemon juice
2 tablespoons honey
2 tablespoons soy sauce
1 clove garlic, minced
¼ teaspoon pepper
2 teaspoons cornstarch
1 tablespoon cooking oil
1 10-ounce package frozen
    cut asparagus, thawed
5 green onions, bias-sliced
    into 1-inch lengths (1 cup)
1 cup cashews
    Hot cooked rice

● Cut chicken into 1-inch pieces. For marinade, stir together water, lemon juice, honey, soy sauce, garlic, and pepper. Add chicken, stirring to coat well. Cover and marinate at room temperature for 30 minutes or in the refrigerator for 2 hours, stirring occasionally. Drain chicken, reserving ½ cup marinade. Stir cornstarch into reserved marinade. Set aside.

● Preheat a wok or large skillet over high heat; add cooking oil. (Add more oil as necessary during cooking.) Stir-fry asparagus in hot oil for 1½ minutes. Add green onions; stir-fry about 1½ minutes or till vegetables are crisp-tender. Remove vegetables from the wok or skillet.

● Add *half* of the chicken to the hot wok or skillet. Stir-fry about 3 minutes or till done. Remove chicken. Stir-fry remaining chicken about 3 minutes. Return all chicken to the wok. Push chicken from center of the wok.

● Stir marinade mixture; add to center of the wok. Cook and stir till thickened and bubbly. Cook and stir for 1 minute more. Return vegetables to the wok; stir ingredients together to coat with marinade mixture. Cook and stir for 1 minute. Stir in cashews. Serve immediately over rice. Makes 4 servings.

Storage Tips

Many oriental ingredients, which are so popular in stir-fried dishes, keep well, if stored correctly.

● Dried ingredients, such as dried mushrooms and lily buds, will keep for several months if stored in an airtight jar or plastic container in a dark, cool, dry place.

● Opened jars or cans of sauces and pastes—such as bean sauce, oyster sauce, and hoisin sauce—will keep for several months if refrigerated. Transfer canned products to airtight containers.

● To store canned water chestnuts and fresh tofu (bean curd), immerse in water; cover and refrigerate, changing water daily. When stored in this manner, tofu and water chestnuts will keep for several weeks.

● For short-term storage of gingerroot, wrap the root in a paper towel and refrigerate. For longer storage, put slices in a container of dry sherry. Cover and refrigerate for up to 3 months.

Planning a Stir-Fry Participation Party

Next time you're planning a dinner party, opt for a stir-fry extravaganza where your guests become participants. Involving your guests in the meal preparation will make it easier for you. And, best of all, it's an icebreaker hard to match.

Although the menu is entirely up to you, here is a possible plan for six persons:

You'll notice that the menu includes two main dishes. This adds variety and keeps the quantity of each dish manageable for stir-frying. You'll need two woks or large skillets, so you might need to ask a guest to bring one. Electric woks work especially well because the participants can stir-fry the dishes right at the table.

Who Brings What

When inviting the guests, assign them ingredients that are easy to transport, and tell them how to prepare them. Use these tips to help you organize your co-op party: (1) Have one guest bring the chicken for Chicken Aloha. (2) Another person can bring the fruit plate. (3) Someone else can bring vegetables for Chicken Aloha. (4) Ask a fourth participant to bring fortune cookies and vegetables for Peppery Beef. (5) Finally, have a fifth guest bring chilled Chinese beer and the chow mein noodles.

You can prepare the difficult-to-transport ingredients—the tea, Egg

Menu

Egg Drop Soup
(see recipe, opposite)

Chicken Aloha
(see recipe, page 35)

Peppery Beef
(see recipe, page 19)

Fruit Plate
(kiwifruit, grapes,
apples, peaches,
and plums)

Purchased Fortune
Cookies

Tea or Chinese Beer

Drop Soup, sauce for Chicken Aloha, and beef and marinade for Peppery Beef. Also, it will be easiest if you rehydrate the dried mushrooms and lily buds for the Peppery Beef.

Party Countdown

To make your party run without a hitch, use the following timetable as a guide. You'll need to prepare the foods for each course just before you eat them so everybody can dine together.

3 to 4 hours before: Set the table and arrange flowers around the room. Prepare the sauce for Chicken Aloha; refrigerate.

2 hours before: For Peppery Beef, prepare the beef and marinade. Marinate in the refrigerator for 2 hours. Rehydrate the dried mushrooms and lily buds.

30 minutes before: For the Egg Drop Soup, in a saucepan slowly stir two 14½-ounce cans *chicken broth* into 1 tablespoon *cornstarch*. Cook, stirring constantly, till slightly thickened. Slowly pour in 1 well-beaten *egg;* stir gently. Keep warm. Prepare tea. As guests arrive, arrange the ingredients they bring for Peppery Beef and for Chicken Aloha on two platters. Warm chow mein noodles.

At serving time: Serve soup in bowls. Garnish with 2 tablespoons sliced *green onion.* Serve beverages.

For the next course, two guests can clear the table and refill beverages while two other guests stir-fry the main dishes side by side.

Clear the table; refill beverages. Finish your meal by having one of the guests serve the fruit plate and fortune cookies.

Fish and Seafood

Cod Stir-Fry

Oriental-style frozen mixed vegetables contain green beans, broccoli, mushrooms, and onions.

1 16-ounce package frozen cod fillets, thawed
2 tablespoons dry sherry
2 tablespoons soy sauce
2 teaspoons cornstarch
¼ teaspoon crushed red pepper
1 tablespoon cooking oil
1 clove garlic, minced
½ of a 16-ounce package (2 cups) loose pack oriental frozen mixed vegetables, thawed
1 small green pepper, cut into thin strips (¾ cup)
¼ cup chopped peanuts
   Hot cooked rice

● Cut fish into 1-inch cubes. For sauce, stir together sherry, soy sauce, cornstarch, red pepper, and ¼ cup *cold water*. Set aside.
● Preheat a wok or large skillet over high heat; add cooking oil. (Add more cooking oil as necessary during cooking.) Stir-fry garlic in hot oil for 15 seconds. Add mixed vegetables; stir-fry for 1½ minutes. Add green pepper; stir-fry about 1½ minutes or till the vegetables are crisp-tender. Remove the vegetables from the wok or skillet.
● Add *half* of the fish to the hot wok. Stir-fry for 3 to 5 minutes or till fish flakes easily, being careful not to break up pieces. Gently remove fish from the wok. Stir-fry remaining fish for 3 to 5 minutes. Gently remove fish from the wok.
● Stir sauce; add to the wok. Cook and stir till thickened and bubbly. Cook and stir for 1 minute more. Return fish and vegetables to the wok; add peanuts. Gently stir ingredients together to coat with sauce. Cover and cook for 1 minute. Serve immediately over hot cooked rice. Makes 4 servings.

Tuna and Rice Stir-Fry

Here's a great way to use leftover rice. If you need to start from scratch, however, keep in mind that for 2 cups of cooked rice you will need ⅔ cup long grain rice or 1 cup quick-cooking rice.

2 tablespoons soy sauce
½ teaspoon finely shredded lemon peel
1 tablespoon cooking oil
2 slightly beaten eggs
1 tablespoon cooking oil
1 clove garlic, minced
2 medium carrots, thinly bias sliced (1 cup)
5 green onions, bias-sliced into 1-inch lengths (1 cup)
1 small green pepper, cut into ¾-inch pieces (½ cup)
2 cups chilled cooked rice
1 6½-ounce can tuna, drained
¼ cup snipped parsley *or* coriander

● For sauce, stir together soy sauce, lemon peel, and ⅛ teaspoon *pepper*. Set aside.
● Preheat a wok or large skillet over medium heat; add 1 tablespoon cooking oil. Add eggs; lift and tilt the wok or skillet to form a thin layer of egg. Cook, without stirring, for 2 to 3 minutes or till just set. Remove from heat; use a spatula to cut into bite-size strips. Remove cooked egg strips from the wok.
● Return the wok to heat. Add 1 tablespoon oil to the hot wok or skillet. (Add more oil as necessary during cooking.) Stir-fry garlic in hot oil over high heat for 15 seconds. Add carrot; stir-fry for 2½ minutes. Add green onions and green pepper; stir-fry about 1½ minutes or till vegetables are crisp-tender.
● Stir sauce and chilled cooked rice into vegetables. Cook and stir for 1 minute. Stir in egg strips, tuna, and parsley. Cover and cook for 1 minute. Serve immediately. Makes 4 servings.

Crab and Pork Stir-Fry

Prevent the crab from shredding into small pieces by gently stirring it into the pork mixture.

½ pound pork tenderloin
1 6-ounce package frozen crab meat, thawed
1 cup chicken broth
2 tablespoons soy sauce
1 tablespoon cornstarch
1 tablespoon dry sherry
1 tablespoon cooking oil
2 cloves garlic, minced
2 medium carrots, thinly bias sliced (1 cup)
2 cups fresh pea pods *or* one 6-ounce package frozen pea pods, thawed
Hot cooked rice

● Partially freeze pork; cut on the bias into thin slices. Cut crab into bite-size pieces. For sauce, stir together chicken broth, soy sauce, cornstarch, and sherry. Set aside.
● Preheat a wok or large skillet over high heat; add cooking oil. (Add more oil as necessary during cooking.) Stir-fry garlic in hot oil for 15 seconds. Add carrots; stir-fry for 2 minutes. Add pea pods; stir-fry about 2 minutes or till vegetables are crisp-tender. Remove vegetables from the wok.
● Add all the pork to the hot wok or skillet. Stir-fry pork about 3 minutes or till no longer pink. Push pork from center of the wok or skillet.
● Stir sauce; add to center of the wok or skillet. Cook and stir till thickened and bubbly. Cook and stir for 2 minutes more. Return vegetables to the wok or skillet; stir ingredients together to coat with sauce. Gently stir in crab. Cover and cook for 1 minute. Serve immediately over rice. Makes 4 servings.

Scallops and Grapes

The sweetness of the currant jelly complements the tartness of lemon juice in this fruity stir-fry.

1 pound fresh *or* frozen scallops
⅓ cup cold water
3 tablespoons currant jelly
2 tablespoons lemon juice
2 teaspoons cornstarch
1 teaspoon instant chicken bouillon granules
1 tablespoon cooking oil
6 ounces fresh mushrooms, sliced (2 cups)
½ pound seedless red *or* green grapes, halved (1⅓ cups)
Hot cooked rice

● Thaw scallops, if frozen. Cut any large scallops into bite-size pieces. For sauce, stir together water, currant jelly, lemon juice, cornstarch, and bouillon granules. Set aside.
● Preheat a wok or large skillet over high heat; add cooking oil. (Add more oil as necessary during cooking.) Stir-fry mushrooms about 1 minute or till done. Remove mushrooms from the wok or skillet.
● Add *half* of the scallops to the hot wok or skillet. Stir-fry scallops for 2 to 3 minutes or till opaque. Remove scallops. Stir-fry remaining scallops for 2 to 3 minutes or till opaque. Remove scallops from the wok or skillet.
● Stir sauce; add to the wok. Cook and stir till thickened and bubbly. Cook and stir for 1 minute more. Return scallops and mushrooms to the wok or skillet; stir ingredients together to coat with sauce. Stir in grapes. Cover and cook for 1 minute. Serve immediately over hot cooked rice. Makes 4 servings.

Lime Scallops Amandine

The size of the food you stir-fry affects its cooking time. For this dish, if you use sea scallops, instead of the smaller bay scallops, halve or quarter them before stir-frying.

1 pound fresh *or* frozen
   scallops
1 cup cold water
½ teaspoon finely shredded
   lime peel
3 tablespoons lime juice
2 tablespoons cornstarch
1 teaspoon sugar
1 teaspoon salt
1 teaspoon instant chicken
   bouillon granules
1 medium cucumber, very
   thinly sliced
1 tablespoon cooking oil
½ pound fresh broccoli,
   cut up (2 cups) (see tip,
   page 67)
1 medium sweet red *or*
   green pepper, cut into
   ¾-inch pieces (¾ cup)
¼ cup sliced almonds

● Thaw scallops, if frozen. Cut any large scallops into bite-size pieces. For sauce, stir together water, lime peel, lime juice, cornstarch, sugar, salt, chicken bouillon granules, and ⅛ teaspoon *pepper.* Set aside. Arrange cucumber slices on a serving platter. Set aside.
● Preheat a wok or large skillet over high heat; add cooking oil. (Add more oil as necessary during cooking.) Stir-fry broccoli in hot oil for 1½ minutes. Add sweet red or green pepper; stir-fry about 1½ minutes or till vegetables are crisp-tender. Remove vegetables from the wok.
● Add *half* of the scallops to the hot wok or skillet. Stir-fry scallops for 2 to 3 minutes or till opaque. Remove scallops. Stir-fry remaining scallops for 2 to 3 minutes or till opaque. Remove scallops from the wok.
● Stir sauce; add to the wok or skillet. Cook and stir till thickened and bubbly. Cook and stir for 2 minutes more. Return scallops and vegetables to the wok; stir ingredients together to coat with sauce. Cook and stir for 1 minute. Stir in almonds. Serve immediately atop cucumber slices. Makes 4 servings.

Shrimp and Apple Stir-Fry

When a recipe calls for chicken broth, you may use homemade broth, canned broth, or bouillon. Canned broth and bouillon will add more salt to the dish, however.

1 pound fresh *or* frozen
   shrimp in shells
¼ cup dry sherry
¼ cup chicken broth
2 teaspoons cornstarch
1 tablespoon cooking oil
5 green onions, bias-sliced
   into 1-inch lengths (1 cup)
2 small red apples, sliced into
   thin wedges (1½ cups)
6 ounces seedless green
   grapes, halved (1 cup)

● Thaw shrimp, if frozen. Shell and devein shrimp (see page 52). Halve shrimp lengthwise. (If shrimp are large, halve again crosswise.) For sauce, stir together sherry, chicken broth, and cornstarch. Set aside.
● Preheat a wok or large skillet over high heat; add cooking oil. (Add more oil as necessary during cooking.) Stir-fry green onions in hot oil about 1½ minutes or till crisp-tender. Remove green onions from the wok or skillet.
● Add *half* of the shrimp to the hot wok or skillet. Stir-fry shrimp for 2 to 3 minutes or till shrimp turn pink. Remove shrimp. Stir-fry remaining shrimp for 2 to 3 minutes. Return all shrimp to the wok. Push shrimp from center of the wok.
● Stir sauce; add to center of the wok or skillet. Cook and stir till thickened and bubbly. Cook and stir for 1 minute more. Return green onions; stir ingredients together to coat with sauce. Stir in apple slices and halved grapes. Cover and cook for 1 minute. Serve immediately. Makes 4 servings.

Lime Scallops Amandine

Surf-and-Turf Stir-Fry

Spinach adds rich color to this gingery beef and shrimp stir-fry.

½ pound beef top round steak
½ pound fresh *or* frozen
    shrimp in shells
2 medium carrots, roll
    cut (1 cup)
¼ cup dry sherry
2 tablespoons cold water
2 tablespoons soy sauce
2 teaspoons cornstarch
1 teaspoon sugar
    Deep-Fried Rice Sticks
1 tablespoon cooking oil
½ teaspoon grated gingerroot
½ pound spinach, torn (6 cups)
1 cup fresh bean sprouts

● Partially freeze beef; cut on the bias into thin bite-size strips. Thaw shrimp, if frozen. Shell and devein shrimp (see page 52). Halve shrimp lengthwise. (If shrimp are large, halve again crosswise.) Cook carrots, covered, in a small amount of boiling salted water for 3½ minutes; drain. For sauce, stir together sherry, water, soy sauce, cornstarch, and sugar. Set aside. Prepare Deep-Fried Rice Sticks; keep warm in oven.

● Preheat a wok or large skillet over high heat; add cooking oil. (Add more oil as necessary during cooking.) Stir-fry gingerroot in hot oil for 15 seconds. Add carrots and spinach; stir-fry for 2 minutes. Add bean sprouts; stir-fry about 1 minute or till vegetables are crisp-tender. Remove vegetables from the wok.

● Add all the beef to the hot wok or skillet. Stir-fry for 2 to 3 minutes or till done. Remove beef. Stir-fry all the shrimp for 2 to 3 minutes or till shrimp turn pink. Return beef. Push beef and shrimp from center of the wok.

● Stir sauce; add to center of the wok. Cook and stir till thickened and bubbly. Cook and stir for 1 minute more. Return vegetables to wok; stir ingredients together to coat. Cook and stir for 1 minute. Serve immediately with rice sticks. Serves 4.

Deep-Fried Rice Sticks: Fry 2 ounces unsoaked *rice sticks,* a few at a time, in deep hot *cooking oil* (375°) about 5 seconds or just till sticks puff and rise to top. Remove rice sticks; drain on a paper towel.

Calorie-Reduced Stir-Frying

Stir-frying enables you to bring to your table a feast that is naturally low in calories—a feast abounding in the fresh goodness of vegetables and lean meats.

Here's a trick to make the most of this low-calorie potential by reducing the amount of oil used in stir-frying. Before you begin cooking, spray an unheated wok or skillet with nonstick vegetable coating. Then preheat the wok or skillet over high heat and begin stir-frying as usual.

When you need more oil to prevent the food from sticking, add cooking oil as necessary. Since you should *never* spray nonstick vegetable coating onto a hot surface, you'll have to use cooking oil after the first spraying.

Mariner's Stir-Fry

This shrimp-and-asparagus stir-fry is elegant enough for company.

1 pound fresh *or* frozen
    shrimp in shells
⅓ cup cold water
¼ cup dry white wine
2 tablespoons soy sauce
1 tablespoon cornstarch
1 tablespoon cooking oil
1 teaspoon grated gingerroot
¾ pound asparagus, bias-
    sliced into 1-inch lengths
    (1½ cups)
5 ounces fresh mushrooms,
    sliced (1 cup)
½ of an 8-ounce can
    (½ cup) sliced water
    chestnuts, drained
8 cherry tomatoes, halved
    Hot cooked brown rice

● Thaw shrimp, if frozen. Shell and devein shrimp (see page 52). Halve shrimp lengthwise. (If shrimp are large, halve again crosswise.) For marinade, stir together water, wine, and soy sauce. Add shrimp, stirring to coat well. Cover and marinate at room temperature for 30 minutes or in the refrigerator for 2 hours, stirring occasionally. Drain shrimp, reserving the marinade. Stir cornstarch into reserved marinade. Set aside.

● Preheat a wok or large skillet over high heat; add cooking oil. (Add more oil as necessary during cooking.) Stir-fry gingerroot in hot oil for 15 seconds. Add asparagus; stir-fry for 4 minutes. Add mushrooms; stir-fry about 1 minute or till asparagus is crisp-tender. Remove vegetables from the wok.

● Add *half* of the shrimp to the hot wok or skillet. Stir-fry for 2 to 3 minutes or till shrimp turn pink. Remove shrimp. Stir-fry remaining shrimp for 2 to 3 minutes or till shrimp turn pink. Return all shrimp to the wok. Stir in water chestnuts. Push shrimp mixture from center of the wok.

● Stir marinade mixture; add to center of the wok. Cook and stir till bubbly. Cook and stir for 1 minute more. Return vegetables; stir ingredients together. Arrange tomatoes atop. Cover and cook for 1 minute. Serve at once atop rice. Makes 4 servings.

Five Spice Shrimp

The shrimp takes on the rich, brown color of the sauce.

1 pound fresh *or* frozen
    shrimp in shells
3 tablespoons teriyaki sauce
½ teaspoon five spice powder
¼ cup dry white wine
2 teaspoons cornstarch
1 tablespoon cooking oil
1 clove garlic, minced
3 stalks celery, thinly
    bias sliced (1½ cups)
1 9-ounce package frozen
    French-style green beans,
    thawed
8 cherry tomatoes, halved

● Thaw shrimp, if frozen. Shell and devein shrimp (see page 52). Halve shrimp lengthwise. (If shrimp are large, halve again crosswise.) Combine teriyaki sauce and five spice powder. Stir in shrimp to coat well. Let stand at room temperature for 15 minutes. Meanwhile, for sauce, stir together wine and cornstarch. Set aside.

● Preheat a wok or large skillet over high heat; add cooking oil. (Add more oil as necessary during cooking.) Stir-fry garlic in hot oil for 15 seconds. Add celery; stir-fry for 1½ minutes. Add green beans; stir-fry about 1½ minutes or till vegetables are crisp-tender. Remove vegetables from the wok.

● Add *half* of the shrimp mixture to the hot wok. Stir-fry for 2 to 3 minutes or till shrimp turn pink. Remove shrimp mixture. Stir-fry remaining shrimp mixture for 2 to 3 minutes. Return all shrimp mixture. Push mixture away from center.

● Stir sauce; add to center of the wok. Cook and stir till thickened and bubbly. Cook and stir for 30 seconds more. Return vegetables; stir ingredients together. Add tomatoes. Cover and cook for 1 minute. Serve immediately. Makes 4 servings.

1 Shelling shrimp

To shell shrimp, use your fingers to open the shell lengthwise down the underside of the body. Hold the shrimp in one hand and carefully peel back the shell, starting with the head end. Leave the last section of the shell and tail intact. Gently pull on the tail to remove the entire shell and tail section.

2 Deveining shrimp

To remove the sandy black vein in the shrimp, first make a shallow slit with a sharp knife along the back of the shrimp. Look for the vein that appears as a dark line running down the center of the back. If it is present, use the tip of the knife to scrape it out and discard it.

Shrimp Creole Stir-Fry

Creole cooking combines the best of French cuisine with spicy Spanish seasonings and incorporates foods readily available in Louisiana and the Gulf States.

1½ pounds fresh *or* frozen shrimp in shells
1 16-ounce can stewed tomatoes
2 tablespoons snipped parsley
2 tablespoons tomato paste
1 tablespoon cornstarch
½ teaspoon bottled hot pepper sauce
1 tablespoon cooking oil
2 cloves garlic, minced
⅛ teaspoon dried thyme, crushed
Dash ground cloves
2 stalks celery, thinly bias sliced (1 cup)
1 medium onion, chopped
1 medium green pepper, chopped (¾ cup)
1 10-ounce package frozen cut okra, thawed
Hot cooked rice

● Thaw shrimp, if frozen. Shell and devein shrimp (see opposite). Halve shrimp lengthwise. (If shrimp are large, halve again crosswise.) For sauce, stir together *undrained* stewed tomatoes, parsley, tomato paste, cornstarch, hot pepper sauce, and ⅓ cup *cold water*. Set aside.

● Preheat a wok or large skillet over high heat; add cooking oil. (Add more oil as necessary during cooking.) Stir-fry garlic, thyme, and cloves in hot oil for 15 seconds. Add celery and onion; stir-fry for 1½ minutes. Add green pepper; stir-fry about 1½ minutes or till vegetables are crisp-tender. Remove vegetables from the wok.

● Add okra to the hot wok or skillet; stir-fry about 3 minutes or till crisp-tender. Remove okra from the wok.

● Add *half* of the shrimp to the hot wok or skillet. Stir-fry for 2 to 3 minutes or till shrimp turns pink. Remove shrimp. Stir-fry the remaining shrimp for 2 to 3 minutes. Remove shrimp.

● Stir sauce; add to the wok. Cook and stir till thickened and bubbly. Cook and stir for 2 minutes more. Return vegetables and okra; stir ingredients together to coat with sauce. Reduce heat. Cover and cook for 3 minutes. Stir in shrimp. Cover and cook for 1 minute. Serve immediately over rice. If desired, pass additional hot pepper sauce. Makes 6 servings.

Shrimp with Hoisin Sauce

You may use one 10-ounce package of frozen cut asparagus instead of fresh asparagus. If you do, thaw the asparagus first, then stir-fry it for only 1½ minutes before adding the green onions.

1 pound fresh *or* frozen shrimp in shells
3 tablespoons cold water
2 tablespoons dry sherry
2 tablespoons hoisin sauce
1 teaspoon cornstarch
1 tablespoon cooking oil
1 pound asparagus, bias-sliced into 1-inch lengths (2 cups)
5 green onions, bias-sliced into 1-inch lengths (1 cup)
1 8-ounce can bamboo shoots, drained

● Thaw shrimp, if frozen. Shell and devein shrimp (see opposite). Halve shrimp lengthwise. (If shrimp are large, halve again crosswise.) For sauce, stir together water, sherry, hoisin sauce, and cornstarch. Set aside.

● Preheat a wok or large skillet over high heat; add cooking oil. (Add more oil as necessary during cooking.) Stir-fry asparagus in hot oil for 5 minutes. Add green onions; stir-fry about 1½ minutes or till vegetables are crisp-tender. Remove vegetables.

● Add *half* of the shrimp to the hot wok. Stir-fry for 2 to 3 minutes or till shrimp turns pink. Remove shrimp. Stir-fry remaining shrimp for 2 to 3 minutes. Return all shrimp to the wok. Stir in bamboo shoots. Push shrimp mixture from center.

● Stir sauce; add to center of the wok. Cook and stir till thickened and bubbly. Cook and stir for 1 minute more. Return vegetables; stir ingredients together to coat with sauce. Cook and stir for 1 minute. Serve immediately. Makes 4 servings.

Meatless

Broccoli-Bulgur Stir-Fry

Look for bulgur wheat in your supermarket or health food store.

1	tablespoon instant beef bouillon granules
1	cup bulgur wheat
3	tablespoons soy sauce
2	teaspoons cornstarch
¼	teaspoon grated lemon peel
1	tablespoon cooking oil
1	clove garlic, minced
2	carrots, thinly sliced
1	pound fresh broccoli, cut up (4 cups) (see tip, page 67)
2	green onions, sliced (¼ cup)
1	cup unsalted peanuts
1	cup shredded mozzarella cheese (4 ounces)

● In a saucepan bring 2 cups *water* to boiling. Add the bouillon granules; stir till dissolved. Remove saucepan from heat. Stir in the bulgur wheat and let stand for 1 hour; drain. Set aside. For sauce, stir together soy sauce, cornstarch, lemon peel, and ⅓ cup *cold water*. Set aside.

● Preheat a wok or large skillet over high heat; add cooking oil. (Add more oil as necessary during cooking.) Stir-fry garlic in hot oil for 15 seconds. Add carrots; stir-fry for 1 minute. Add broccoli; stir-fry for 1½ minutes. Add green onions; stir-fry about 1½ minutes or till vegetables are crisp-tender. Push vegetables from center of the wok or skillet.

● Stir sauce; add to center of the wok. Cook and stir till bubbly. Cook and stir for 1 minute more. Stir in vegetables and bulgur mixture to coat with sauce. Cook and stir for 1 minute. Stir in peanuts. Sprinkle with cheese. Serve at once. Makes 4 servings.

Vegetarian Chow Mein

Peanuts add crunch to this saucy vegetable-and-tofu mixture served over crisp noodles.

4	dried mushrooms
2	tablespoons dry white wine
1	tablespoon soy sauce
2	teaspoons cornstarch
½	teaspoon instant chicken bouillon granules
1	tablespoon cooking oil
1	teaspoon grated gingerroot
1	cup sliced cauliflower
2	medium carrots, thinly bias sliced (1 cup)
1	10-ounce package frozen peas, thawed
½	of a 14-ounce can (1 cup) bean sprouts, drained
8	ounces fresh tofu (bean curd), cut into ½-inch cubes (1½ cups)
1	cup peanuts, chopped
	Warm chow mein noodles

● Soak mushrooms in enough warm water to cover about 30 minutes or till rehydrated (see page 19). Squeeze to drain thoroughly. Thinly slice mushrooms, discarding the stems. Meanwhile, for sauce, stir together wine, soy sauce, cornstarch, bouillon granules, and ½ cup *cold water*. Set aside.

● Preheat a wok or large skillet over high heat; add cooking oil. (Add more oil as necessary during cooking.) Stir-fry gingerroot in hot oil for 15 seconds. Add cauliflower; stir-fry for 1 minute. Add carrots; stir-fry about 4 minutes or till vegetables are crisp-tender. Stir in mushrooms, peas, and bean sprouts. Push vegetables from center of the wok.

● Stir sauce; add to center of the wok or skillet. Cook and stir till thickened and bubbly. Cook and stir for 1 minute more. Stir in vegetables to coat with sauce. Gently stir in tofu. Cover and cook for 1 minute. Stir in peanuts. Serve immediately over warm chow mein noodles. Makes 4 servings.

Tofu Primavera

Napa cabbage, also called Chinese cabbage and celery cabbage, is a common ingredient in Chinese stir-frys. It has an elongated head with white stalks and crinkled, pale green leaves.

½ cup cold water
¼ cup soy sauce
1 tablespoon cornstarch
2 teaspoons sugar
⅛ teaspoon crushed red pepper
1 tablespoon cooking oil
2 cloves garlic, minced
3 medium carrots, thinly bias sliced (1½ cups)
5 green onions, bias-sliced into 1-inch lengths (1 cup)
1 medium green pepper, cut into thin strips (1 cup)
3 cups thinly sliced Napa cabbage
8 ounces fresh tofu (bean curd), cut into ½-inch cubes (1½ cups)
1 medium tomato, cut into thin wedges
¾ cup unsalted peanuts

● For sauce, stir together water, soy sauce, cornstarch, sugar, and crushed red pepper. Set aside.

● Preheat a wok or large skillet over high heat; add cooking oil. (Add more oil as necessary during cooking.) Stir-fry garlic in hot oil for 15 seconds. Add carrots; stir-fry for 2½ minutes. Add green onions and green pepper; stir-fry about 1½ minutes or till vegetables are crisp-tender. Push vegetables from center of the wok or skillet.

● Stir sauce; add to center of the wok or skillet. Cook and stir till thickened and bubbly. Cook and stir for 2 minutes more. Stir in vegetables to coat with sauce. Gently stir in Napa cabbage, fresh tofu, and tomato wedges. Cover and cook for 1 minute. Gently stir in peanuts. Serve immediately. Makes 4 servings.

Using Tofu in Stir-Fries

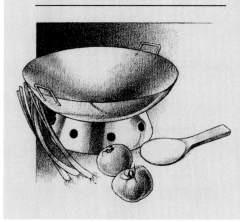

Tofu or bean curd, with its high protein content, is a common meat substitute in meatless main dishes. This custardlike food is made from boiled soybean milk. Nearly flavorless, tofu complements many foods and tends to pick up the other seasonings in a dish.

You can usually find tofu in the produce section of your supermarket. Be sure to purchase tofu that has been refrigerated or delivered fresh daily. Turn to the tip on page 43 for information on storing tofu.

To prepare tofu for stir-fried dishes, drain and cut into bite-size cubes. Because tofu is precooked and needs no further cooking and because it is delicate and may break into small pieces, add it at the end of stir-frying. Gently stir into other ingredients.

Vegetable-Pasta Stir-Fry

Vegetable-Pasta Stir-Fry

Here's a hearty main dish that combines lots of fresh vegetables, pasta, and cheese.

6 ounces linguine, broken up
1 tablespoon cooking oil
2 cloves garlic, minced
2 medium carrots, thinly
 bias sliced (1 cup)
1 medium zucchini, thinly
 sliced (1¼ cups)
1 medium onion, chopped
1 stalk celery, thinly sliced
1 15-ounce can garbanzo
 beans, drained
3 medium tomatoes, chopped
½ cup sliced pitted ripe olives
¼ cup snipped parsley
1 tablespoon snipped fresh
 basil *or* 1 teaspoon dried
 basil, crushed
¼ cup grated Parmesan cheese
3 tablespoons butter
1 cup shredded mozzarella
 cheese (4 ounces)

● Cook linguine in boiling *unsalted* water according to package directions; drain. Keep warm.

● Meanwhile, preheat a wok or large skillet over high heat; add cooking oil. (Add more oil as necessary during cooking.) Stir-fry garlic in hot oil for 15 seconds. Add carrots; stir-fry for 2 minutes. Add zucchini, onion, and celery; stir-fry about 3 minutes or till vegetables are crisp-tender.

● Gently stir in garbanzo beans, tomatoes, olives, snipped parsley, and basil. Cover and cook for 1 to 2 minutes or till mixture is heated through.

● Remove the wok or skillet from heat. Add linguine, Parmesan cheese, and butter. Toss gently till mixture is coated. Transfer to 4 dinner plates; sprinkle mozzarella cheese over each serving. Garnish with fresh basil, if desired. Serve immediately. Makes 4 servings.

Vegetarian Fried Rice

You may wish to pass additional soy sauce with this harvest-of-vegetables fried rice.

1 tablespoon dry sherry
1 tablespoon soy sauce
½ teaspoon sugar
 Dash bottled hot pepper
 sauce
1 tablespoon cooking oil
2 beaten eggs
1 tablespoon cooking oil
1 clove garlic, minced
1 medium cucumber, seeded
 and chopped (1 cup)
1 small onion, chopped
1 small green pepper, coarsely
 chopped (½ cup)
3 cups chilled, cooked rice
2 medium tomatoes, chopped
½ cup peanuts
½ cup shredded cheddar
 cheese (2 ounces)

● For sauce, stir together sherry, soy sauce, sugar, hot pepper sauce, and 1 tablespoon *water.* Set aside.

● Preheat a wok or large skillet over medium heat; add 1 tablespoon oil. Add eggs; lift and tilt the wok or skillet to form a thin layer of egg. Cook eggs, without stirring, for 2 to 3 minutes or till just set. Remove wok from heat. Use a spatula to cut the eggs into bite-size strips. Remove egg strips from the wok.

● Return the wok to heat. Add 1 tablespoon oil to the hot wok or skillet. (Add more oil as necessary during cooking.) Stir-fry garlic in hot oil over high heat for 15 seconds. Add cucumber and onion; stir-fry for 1½ minutes. Add green pepper; stir-fry about 1½ minutes more or till vegetables are crisp-tender.

● Stir sauce and chilled rice into vegetables. Cook and stir for 1 minute. Gently stir in egg strips and tomatoes. Cover and cook for 1 minute. Stir in peanuts. Transfer rice mixture to a serving bowl; sprinkle with cheddar cheese. Serve immediately. Makes 4 servings.

CREATE A STIR

Throw yourself wholeheartedly into
mix-and-match stir-frying.
To help you, here are three recipes
that give you options for fresh,
frozen, or leftover ingredients.
You'll also find a chart containing
stir-fry timings for 14
different vegetables. What a great help
when you get the urge to venture
out on your own!

Sherried Stir-Fry

From the fresh vegetable options listed below, select your favorites that are in season.

1 pound Fresh Meat Option
3 tablespoons water
3 tablespoons dry sherry
¼ cup Broth Option
1 tablespoon cornstarch
1 tablespoon soy sauce
½ teaspoon sugar
    Seasoning Option
1 tablespoon cooking oil
1½ cups Fresh Vegetable
    Option 1
1½ cups Fresh Vegetable
    Option 2

● If using beef or pork as the Meat Option, partially freeze the meat; cut on the bias into thin bite-size strips. If using chicken, cut the meat into 1-inch pieces.

● For marinade, stir together water and sherry. Add meat, stirring to coat well. Cover and marinate at room temperature for 30 minutes or in the refrigerator for 2 hours, stirring occasionally. Drain meat, reserving marinade. For sauce, stir together reserved marinade, Broth Option, cornstarch, soy sauce, sugar, and Seasoning Option. Set aside.

● Preheat a wok or large skillet over high heat; add cooking oil. (Add more oil as necessary during cooking.) Stir-fry Vegetable Option 1 in hot oil for 2 minutes. Add Vegetable Option 2; stir-fry about 3 minutes or till vegetables are crisp-tender. Remove vegetables from the wok or skillet.

● Add *half* of the meat to the hot wok or skillet. Stir-fry about 3 minutes or till done. Remove meat. Stir-fry remaining meat about 3 minutes or till done. Return all meat to the wok or skillet. Push meat from center of the wok or skillet.

● Stir sauce; add to center of the wok or skillet. Cook and stir till thickened and bubbly. Cook and stir for 30 seconds more. Return vegetables to the wok or skillet; stir ingredients together to coat with sauce. Cook and stir for 1 minute. Serve immediately. Makes 4 servings.

Fresh Meat Options

beef top round steak
boneless pork
skinned and boned
    chicken breasts

Broth Options

beef broth (for beef)
chicken broth (for pork *or* chicken)

Seasoning Options

½ teaspoon dried basil, crushed
¼ teaspoon dried rosemary, crushed
⅛ teaspoon crushed red pepper

Fresh Vegetable Options 1

thinly bias-sliced carrots
sliced cauliflower
asparagus bias-sliced into
    1-inch lengths

Fresh Vegetable Options 2

thinly sliced zucchini
pea pods, halved diagonally
thinly bias-sliced celery

Fruit-Sauced Stir-Fry

Keep the frozen chicken and the options for the frozen vegetable mixtures and juice concentrates on hand for a quick-to-prepare dinner.

½ cup cold water
2 tablespoons Frozen Juice
  Concentrate Option
1 tablespoon soy sauce
1½ teaspoons cornstarch
½ teaspoon instant chicken
  bouillon granules
½ teaspoon ground ginger
1 tablespoon cooking oil
¼ cup sliced almonds *or*
  chopped peanuts
3 cups loose-pack Frozen
  Mixed Vegetable Option
1 12-ounce package (3 cups)
  frozen diced cooked
  chicken
  Hot cooked rice

● For sauce, stir together water, Frozen Juice Concentrate Option, soy sauce, cornstarch, chicken bouillon granules, and ground ginger. Set aside.

● Preheat a wok or large skillet over high heat; add cooking oil. (Add more oil as necessary during cooking.) If using almonds, stir-fry in hot oil about 1 minute or till lightly toasted; remove from wok (if using peanuts, set aside). Stir-fry Frozen Mixed Vegetable Option in the hot wok for 3 to 4 minutes or till vegetables are crisp-tender. Remove vegetables from wok or skillet.

● Stir-fry frozen chicken in the hot wok about 3 minutes or till heated through. Push chicken from center of the wok.

● Stir sauce; add to center of the wok or skillet. Cook and stir till thickened and bubbly. Cook and stir for 1 minute more. Return vegetables to the wok; stir ingredients together to coat with sauce. Cook and stir for 1 minute. Stir in almonds or peanuts. Serve immediately over hot cooked rice. Makes 4 servings.

Frozen Juice Concentrate Options	**Frozen Mixed Vegetable Options**
orange	green beans, broccoli, onions, and mushrooms
apple	broccoli, carrots, and cauliflower
pineapple	French-cut green beans, broccoli, mushrooms, and sweet red peppers
pineapple-orange	broccoli, carrots, and onions

Oriental Stir-Fry

Even leftovers can be fun when you use them to create a stir-fry. And if you don't have enough of one meat or vegetable to equal 2 cups, mix and match what you have.

½ cup cold water
3 tablespoons soy sauce
1 tablespoon cornstarch
½ teaspoon instant
    Bouillon Granule Option
¼ teaspoon ground ginger
⅛ teaspoon garlic powder
1 tablespoon cooking oil
1 medium green pepper, cut
    into ¾-inch pieces (¾ cup)
3 green onions, cut into
    1-inch lengths (½ cup)
2 cups Cooked Meat Option
2 cups Cooked Vegetable
    Option
    Hot cooked rice

● For sauce, stir together cold water, soy sauce, cornstarch, instant Bouillon Granule Option, ginger, and garlic powder. Set sauce aside.

● Preheat a wok or large skillet over high heat; add cooking oil. (Add more oil as necessary during cooking.) Stir-fry green pepper and green onions in hot oil about 2 minutes or till vegetables are crisp-tender. Push from center of the wok.

● Stir sauce; add to center of the wok. Cook and stir till thickened and bubbly. Cook and stir for 2 minutes more. Add Cooked Meat Option and Cooked Vegetable Option; stir ingredients together to coat with sauce. Cover and cook about 3 minutes or till heated through. Serve immediately over rice. Makes 4 servings.

Bouillon Granule Options	Cooked Meat Options	Cooked Vegetable Options

beef (for beef)
chicken (for pork, lamb,
   chicken, *or* turkey)
	cubed beef
	cubed pork
	cubed lamb
	chicken cut into bite-size
	  strips
	turkey cut into bite-size
	  strips
		sliced carrots
		asparagus bias-sliced into
		  1-inch lengths
		sliced cauliflower
		sliced broccoli
		green beans bias-sliced into
		  1-inch lengths
		peas

Stir-Fried Vegetables

To really show off your stir-fry talents, create your own recipes for stir-fried vegetable side dishes. Here are a few tips and a handy stir-fry timing chart to help you along the way.

When planning a stir-fry, you can learn much from experienced Chinese cooks who have developed stir-frying to a fine art. To the

Chinese, good taste is not enough. A stir-fry must be a harmonious blend of color, taste, and texture. The possibilities for mixing and matching ingredients in a pleasing way are almost limitless. Just keep the qualities you are looking for in mind when choosing the vegetables you will include in your stir-fry.

Once you have selected your ingredients, decide how you will prepare them. You may slice, bias-slice, cut into julienne strips, or roll-cut your vegetables (see "Cutting Terms," pages 8–9). Because the size and shape of the food will affect the stir-fry time, we have included chart entries for vegetables prepared in different ways.

Ingredient	Quantity	Preparation Directions	Stir-Fry Time
Asparagus (fresh)	¾ pound	Remove tough portion of stem; bias-slice into 1-inch lengths (1½ cups).	4 to 5 minutes
Asparagus (frozen)	One 10-ounce package frozen cut asparagus	Thaw.	3 minutes
Bok Choy	½ of a small bunch	Thinly slice (2½ cups).	3 minutes
Broccoli (fresh)	½ pound	Cut flowerets into bite-size pieces; thinly slice stems (2 cups).	3 to 4 minutes
Broccoli (frozen)	One 10-ounce package frozen cut broccoli	Thaw.	2 to 3 minutes
Cabbage	½ of a small head	Core and coarsely shred or chop (3 cups).	3 minutes
Carrots (fresh)	3 medium	Thinly bias-slice (1½ cups).	4 to 5 minutes
	4 medium	Cut into julienne strips (1½ cups).	4 minutes
Cauliflower	½ of a medium head	Remove leaves and stem; thinly slice (2¼ cups).	5 minutes
Celery	3 stalks	Thinly bias-slice (1½ cups).	3 to 4 minutes

Next, consider the quantity of the vegetables you have chosen. Limiting the amount you stir-fry at one time to about 3 cups is a good guideline. Plan on at least ¾ cup uncooked vegetable mixture for each serving. If you want to stir-fry for a crowd, take out a second wok or a large skillet and have a helper stir-fry alongside you.

Now you are ready to start stir-frying (see "Stir-Fry Basics," pages 10–13). Start with the vegetable that will take the most time to stir-fry. Then add the other vegetables as necessary for them to get their recommended amount of cooking time. Stir-fry until vegetables are crisp-tender. If you like, season with soy sauce, lemon juice, salt and pepper, garlic salt, or any other seasoning that strikes your fancy.

Whether you use the vegetable chart to create your own stir-fried side dishes or just as a guide when substituting one vegetable for another, we're sure you'll find it to be a much-used reference.

Ingredient	Quantity	Preparation Directions	Stir-Fry Time
Green Beans (fresh)	½ pound	Bias-slice into 1-inch pieces (1½ cups). Precook, covered, in a small amount of boiling salted water for 4 minutes; drain.	3 minutes
Green Beans (frozen)	One 9-ounce package frozen French-style green beans	Thaw.	1½ minutes
Green Onions	4	Bias-slice into 1-inch lengths (¾ cup).	1½ minutes
Green Pepper	1 medium	Cut into ¾-inch pieces (¾ cup).	1½ minutes
Mushrooms	¼ pound	Slice (1½ cups).	1 minute
Onion	1 medium 1 medium	Chop (½ cup). Slice into thin wedges, or slice and separate into rings.	2 minutes 3 minutes
Pea Pods (fresh)	6 to 8 ounces	Remove tips and strings (3 cups).	2 to 3 minutes
Pea Pods (frozen)	One 6-ounce package frozen pea pods	Thaw.	1 to 2 minutes
Zucchini or Yellow Summer Squash	1 medium	Slice ¼ inch thick (1¼ cups).	3 to 3½ minutes

SIDE DISHES

*Fresh vegetables and stir-frying
are made for each other. Because you
cook the vegetables in a flash, they
stay crisp, colorful, and
wonderfully flavorful. And the
freshness of these side
dishes is a great way to liven up
any type of meat.*

Green Beans with Ham

Ham and onion wedges lend a bit of the South to this stir-fried dish.

½ pound fresh green beans,
  bias-sliced into 1-inch
  pieces (2 cups)
1 tablespoon cooking oil
1 small onion, sliced into
  thin wedges
¼ cup finely chopped fully
  cooked ham

● Cook green beans, covered, in a small amount of boiling salted water for 4 minutes; drain. Preheat a wok or large skillet over high heat; add cooking oil. (Add more oil as necessary during cooking.) Stir-fry green beans and onion wedges in hot oil about 3 minutes or till green beans are crisp-tender.

● Stir in ham. Cook and stir for 1 minute. Sprinkle vegetables with a little salt and pepper, if desired. Serve immediately. Makes 6 servings.

Gingered Green Beans and Cauliflower

The bite in this recipe comes from gingerroot and crushed red pepper.

½ pound fresh green beans,
  bias-sliced into 1-inch
  pieces (2 cups)
2 tablespoons dry sherry
4 teaspoons soy sauce
1½ teaspoons cornstarch
½ teaspoon sugar
½ teaspoon grated gingerroot
⅛ teaspoon crushed red
  pepper
1 tablespoon cooking oil
½ of a small head cauliflower,
  sliced (about 1¾ cups)
2 medium tomatoes, cut into
  thin wedges

● Cook green beans, covered, in a small amount of boiling salted water for 4 minutes; drain. For sauce, stir together dry sherry, soy sauce, cornstarch, sugar, gingerroot, and red pepper. Set sauce aside.

● Preheat a wok or large skillet over high heat; add cooking oil. (Add more oil as necessary during cooking.) Stir-fry cauliflower in hot oil for 2 minutes. Add green beans; stir-fry about 3 minutes or till vegetables are crisp-tender. Push vegetables from center of the wok.

● Stir sauce; add to center of the wok or skillet. Cook and stir till thickened and bubbly. Cook and stir for 15 seconds more. Stir in vegetables to coat with sauce. Arrange tomatoes atop. Cover and cook for 1 minute. Serve immediately. Makes 6 servings.

Basil Green Beans

To substitute a fresh herb for the dried form, you generally use three times more of the fresh herb. In this recipe, use 1½ teaspoons snipped fresh basil.

¾ pound fresh green beans, bias-sliced into 1-inch pieces (3 cups)
⅓ cup plain yogurt
1 teaspoon cornstarch
¼ cup milk
½ teaspoon dried basil, crushed
1 tablespoon cooking oil
¼ cup slivered almonds

● Cook green beans, covered, in a small amount of boiling salted water for 4 minutes; drain. For sauce, stir together yogurt and cornstarch. Stir in milk and basil. Set aside.

● Preheat a wok or large skillet over high heat; add cooking oil. (Add more oil as necessary during cooking.) Stir-fry almonds in hot oil for 30 to 45 seconds or till toasted. Remove almonds from the wok or skillet. Stir-fry green beans in the hot wok about 3 minutes or till crisp-tender. Push green beans from center of the wok or skillet.

● Reduce heat. Add sauce to center of the wok or skillet. Cook and stir till thickened and bubbly. Cook and stir for 30 seconds more. Stir in green beans and almonds to coat with sauce. Serve immediately. Makes 6 servings.

Vegetable-Stick Stir-Fry

Carrots and zucchini, cut into julienne strips, and green beans and green onions, cut into 1-inch lengths, make a colorful stir-fry of stick vegetables.

½ pound fresh green beans, bias-sliced into 1-inch pieces (2 cups)
2 tablespoons cold water
2 tablespoons dry sherry
2 tablespoons soy sauce
2 teaspoons sugar
1½ teaspoons cornstarch
Dash pepper
1 tablespoon cooking oil
2 medium carrots, cut into julienne strips (¾ cup)
1 medium zucchini, cut into julienne strips (2 cups)
6 green onions, bias-sliced into 1-inch lengths (1¼ cups)

● Cook green beans, covered, in a small amount of boiling salted water for 4 minutes; drain. For sauce, stir together cold water, dry sherry, soy sauce, sugar, cornstarch, and pepper. Set sauce aside.

● Preheat a wok or large skillet over high heat; add cooking oil. (Add more oil as necessary during cooking.) Stir-fry carrots in hot oil for 1 minute. Add green beans and zucchini; stir-fry for 1½ minutes. Add green onions; stir-fry about 1½ minutes or till vegetables are crisp-tender. Push vegetables from center of the wok or skillet.

● Stir sauce; add to center of the wok or skillet. Cook and stir till thickened and bubbly. Cook and stir for 30 seconds more. Stir in the vegetables to coat with the sauce. Serve immediately. Makes 6 servings.

Basil Green Beans

To substitute a fresh herb for the dried form, you generally use three times more of the fresh herb. In this recipe, use 1½ teaspoons snipped fresh basil.

¾ pound fresh green beans,
   bias-sliced into 1-inch
   pieces (3 cups)
⅓ cup plain yogurt
1 teaspoon cornstarch
¼ cup milk
½ teaspoon dried basil,
   crushed
1 tablespoon cooking oil
¼ cup slivered almonds

● Cook green beans, covered, in a small amount of boiling salted water for 4 minutes; drain. For sauce, stir together yogurt and cornstarch. Stir in milk and basil. Set aside.

● Preheat a wok or large skillet over high heat; add cooking oil. (Add more oil as necessary during cooking.) Stir-fry almonds in hot oil for 30 to 45 seconds or till toasted. Remove almonds from the wok or skillet. Stir-fry green beans in the hot wok about 3 minutes or till crisp-tender. Push green beans from center of the wok or skillet.

● Reduce heat. Add sauce to center of the wok or skillet. Cook and stir till thickened and bubbly. Cook and stir for 30 seconds more. Stir in green beans and almonds to coat with sauce. Serve immediately. Makes 6 servings.

Vegetable-Stick Stir-Fry

Carrots and zucchini, cut into julienne strips, and green beans and green onions, cut into 1-inch lengths, make a colorful stir-fry of stick vegetables.

½ pound fresh green beans,
   bias-sliced into 1-inch
   pieces (2 cups)
2 tablespoons cold water
2 tablespoons dry sherry
2 tablespoons soy sauce
2 teaspoons sugar
1½ teaspoons cornstarch
   Dash pepper
1 tablespoon cooking oil
2 medium carrots, cut into
   julienne strips (¾ cup)
1 medium zucchini, cut into
   julienne strips (2 cups)
6 green onions, bias-sliced
   into 1-inch lengths
   (1¼ cups)

● Cook green beans, covered, in a small amount of boiling salted water for 4 minutes; drain. For sauce, stir together cold water, dry sherry, soy sauce, sugar, cornstarch, and pepper. Set sauce aside.

● Preheat a wok or large skillet over high heat; add cooking oil. (Add more oil as necessary during cooking.) Stir-fry carrots in hot oil for 1 minute. Add green beans and zucchini; stir-fry for 1½ minutes. Add green onions; stir-fry about 1½ minutes or till vegetables are crisp-tender. Push vegetables from center of the wok or skillet.

● Stir sauce; add to center of the wok or skillet. Cook and stir till thickened and bubbly. Cook and stir for 30 seconds more. Stir in the vegetables to coat with the sauce. Serve immediately. Makes 6 servings.

Green Beans with Ham

Ham and onion wedges lend a bit of the South to this stir-fried dish.

½ pound fresh green beans,
  bias-sliced into 1-inch
  pieces (2 cups)
1 tablespoon cooking oil
1 small onion, sliced into
  thin wedges
¼ cup finely chopped fully
  cooked ham

● Cook green beans, covered, in a small amount of boiling salted water for 4 minutes; drain. Preheat a wok or large skillet over high heat; add cooking oil. (Add more oil as necessary during cooking.) Stir-fry green beans and onion wedges in hot oil about 3 minutes or till green beans are crisp-tender.
● Stir in ham. Cook and stir for 1 minute. Sprinkle vegetables with a little salt and pepper, if desired. Serve immediately. Makes 6 servings.

Gingered Green Beans and Cauliflower

The bite in this recipe comes from gingerroot and crushed red pepper.

½ pound fresh green beans,
  bias-sliced into 1-inch
  pieces (2 cups)
2 tablespoons dry sherry
4 teaspoons soy sauce
1½ teaspoons cornstarch
½ teaspoon sugar
½ teaspoon grated gingerroot
⅛ teaspoon crushed red
  pepper
1 tablespoon cooking oil
½ of a small head cauliflower,
  sliced (about 1¾ cups)
2 medium tomatoes, cut into
  thin wedges

● Cook green beans, covered, in a small amount of boiling salted water for 4 minutes; drain. For sauce, stir together dry sherry, soy sauce, cornstarch, sugar, gingerroot, and red pepper. Set sauce aside.
● Preheat a wok or large skillet over high heat; add cooking oil. (Add more oil as necessary during cooking.) Stir-fry cauliflower in hot oil for 2 minutes. Add green beans; stir-fry about 3 minutes or till vegetables are crisp-tender. Push vegetables from center of the wok.
● Stir sauce; add to center of the wok or skillet. Cook and stir till thickened and bubbly. Cook and stir for 15 seconds more. Stir in vegetables to coat with sauce. Arrange tomatoes atop. Cover and cook for 1 minute. Serve immediately. Makes 6 servings.

Mustard-Sauced Medley

Dijon-style mustard is based on a mustard made in Dijon, France. Its tart, yet pleasing flavor complements the broccoli, carrots, and onion in this stir-fried side dish.

⅓ cup milk
2 teaspoons Dijon-style mustard
1½ teaspoons cornstarch
1 teaspoon instant chicken bouillon granules
1 tablespoon cooking oil
2 medium carrots, thinly bias sliced (1 cup)
¾ pound fresh broccoli, cut up (3 cups) (see tip, page 67)
1 medium onion, thinly sliced and separated into rings

● For sauce, stir together milk, mustard, cornstarch, and bouillon granules. Set aside.

● Preheat a wok or large skillet over high heat; add cooking oil. (Add more oil as necessary during cooking.) Stir-fry carrots in hot oil for 1 minute. Add broccoli and onion; stir-fry about 4 minutes or till vegetables are crisp-tender. Push vegetables from center of the wok.

● Stir sauce; add to center of the wok or skillet. Cook and stir till thickened and bubbly. Cook and stir for 1 minute more. Stir in stir-fried vegetables to coat with the sauce. Serve immediately. Makes 6 servings.

Zucchini and Tomato Parmesan

Popular Italian ingredients, including garlic and Parmesan cheese, make this stir-fried recipe as flavorful as it is colorful.

1 tablespoon cooking oil
1 clove garlic, minced
2 medium zucchini, halved lengthwise and sliced ¼-inch thick (2½ cups)
4 green onions, bias-sliced into 1-inch lengths (¾ cup)
2 medium tomatoes, seeded and chopped (1 cup)
¼ cup snipped parsley
½ cup grated Parmesan *or* Romano cheese

● Preheat a wok or large skillet over high heat; add cooking oil. (Add more oil as necessary during cooking.) Stir-fry garlic in hot oil for 15 seconds. Add zucchini; stir-fry for 1½ minutes. Add green onions; stir-fry about 1½ minutes or till vegetables are crisp-tender.

● Stir in tomatoes and parsley. Cover and cook about 1 minute or till heated through. Sprinkle with Parmesan or Romano cheese; toss gently. Serve immediately. Makes 6 servings.

Ratatouille-Style Stir-Fry

Our stir-fried version of this well-seasoned French vegetable stew includes summer squash, onion, green pepper, and tomatoes.

1	tablespoon snipped parsley
1	tablespoon vinegar
¼	teaspoon dried basil, crushed
¼	teaspoon dried oregano, crushed
1	tablespoon cooking oil
1	clove garlic, minced
2	medium zucchini *or* yellow summer squash, halved lengthwise and bias-sliced ¼ inch thick (2½ cups)
1	small onion, thinly sliced and separated into rings
1	medium green pepper, cut into thin strips (1 cup)
2	medium tomatoes, coarsely chopped (1 cup)

● Stir together snipped parsley, vinegar, basil, and oregano. Set mixture aside.

● Preheat a wok or large skillet over high heat; add cooking oil. (Add more oil as necessary during cooking.) Stir-fry garlic in hot oil for 15 seconds. Add zucchini and onion; stir-fry for 2 minutes. Add green pepper; stir-fry about 2 minutes or till vegetables are crisp-tender.

● Stir vinegar mixture and tomatoes into vegetables. Cover and cook for 1 minute. Sprinkle with a little salt, if desired. Serve immediately. Makes 8 servings.

Squash with Cheese Sauce

Butternut squash, one of several varieties of winter squash, is pear-shaped with a long neck and a smooth, yellow shell. Choose squash that is heavy for its size with a hard rind.

½	cup milk
1½	teaspoons cornstarch
¼	teaspoon dried thyme, crushed
⅛	teaspoon pepper
1	tablespoon cooking oil
1	pound butternut squash, peeled and cut into ¾-inch pieces (2 cups)
1	leek, thinly sliced (¾ cup)
2	slices processed Swiss *or* American cheese, torn into small pieces (2 ounces)

● For sauce, stir together milk, cornstarch, thyme, and pepper. Set aside.

● Preheat a wok or large skillet over high heat; add cooking oil. (Add more oil as necessary during cooking.) Stir-fry squash in hot oil for 2 minutes. Add leek; stir-fry about 1½ minutes or till vegetables are crisp-tender. Push vegetables from center of the wok or skillet.

● Reduce heat. Stir sauce; add to center of the wok or skillet. Cook and stir till thickened and bubbly. Cook and stir for 1 minute more. Stir in vegetables to coat with sauce. Remove from heat. Stir in Swiss or American cheese till melted. Serve immediately. Makes 4 servings.

Hot Spinach Salad

Apple wedges add crunch to this sweet-and-sour spinach salad.

¼ cup apple juice
3 tablespoons wine vinegar
1 tablespoon brown sugar
1½ teaspoons cornstarch
1 tablespoon cooking oil
1 small onion, thinly
   sliced and separated
   into rings
1 small apple, cored and
   sliced into thin wedges
½ cup sliced fresh mushrooms
5 ounces spinach, torn
   (4 cups)
1 hard-cooked egg, sliced

● For sauce, stir together apple juice, wine vinegar, brown sugar, and cornstarch. Set aside.
● Preheat a wok or large skillet over high heat; add cooking oil. (Add more oil as necessary during cooking.) Stir-fry onion in hot oil for 2 minutes. Add apple and mushrooms; stir-fry about 1 minute or till onion is tender. Push the vegetable mixture from center of the wok.
● Stir sauce; add to center of the wok or skillet. Cook and stir till thickened and bubbly. Cook and stir for 1 minute more. Stir in vegetable mixture to coat with sauce. Place spinach in a large salad bowl. Pour hot mixture over spinach. Toss gently till well coated. Top with hard-cooked egg slices. Serve immediately. Makes 3 servings.

Sweet-and-Sour Red Cabbage

The vinegar in this tangy sauce intensifies the color of the red cabbage.

3 tablespoons brown sugar
3 tablespoons cold water
3 tablespoons vinegar
3 tablespoons dry red wine
1½ teaspoons cornstarch
¼ teaspoon salt
   Dash pepper
1 tablespoon cooking oil
½ of a small head red
   cabbage, shredded
   (4 cups)
1 medium onion, chopped
   (½ cup)
1 medium pear *or* apple,
   cored and chopped (1 cup)

● For sauce, stir together brown sugar, water, vinegar, wine, cornstarch, salt, and pepper. Set aside.
● Preheat a wok or large skillet over high heat; add cooking oil. (Add more oil as necessary during cooking.) Stir-fry cabbage in hot oil for 1 minute. Add onion; stir-fry for 1 minute. Add pear or apple; stir-fry about 1 minute or till cabbage is crisp-tender. Push vegetable mixture from center of the wok.
● Stir sauce; add to center of the wok or skillet. Cook and stir till thickened and bubbly. Cook and stir for 1 minute more. Stir in vegetable mixture to coat with sauce. Serve immediately. Makes 4 or 5 servings.

Honey-Orange Sweet Potatoes

Cabbage and Potato Stir-Fry

To make easy work of mincing garlic, place a clove on a cutting board. Use the flat side of a cleaver or knife to press down on the garlic to loosen the peel. Remove peel and finely chop.

3 medium potatoes, peeled and cut into ½-inch cubes (3 cups)
2 tablespoons cold water
2 tablespoons teriyaki sauce
1 tablespoon snipped parsley
½ teaspoon cornstarch
1 tablespoon cooking oil
1 clove garlic, minced
½ of a small head cabbage, shredded (4 cups)
1 small onion, chopped (¼ cup)

● Cook potatoes, covered, in boiling salted water for 4 minutes; drain. For sauce, stir together water, teriyaki sauce, parsley, and cornstarch. Set aside.

● Preheat a wok or large skillet over high heat; add cooking oil. (Add more oil as necessary during cooking.) Stir-fry garlic in hot oil for 15 seconds. Add cabbage; stir-fry for 1 minute. Add onion; stir-fry for 1 minute. Add potatoes; stir-fry about 2 minutes or till cabbage is crisp-tender. Push vegetables from center of the wok or skillet.

● Stir sauce; add to center of the wok or skillet. Cook and stir till thickened and bubbly. Cook and stir for 30 seconds more. Stir in the vegetables to coat with sauce. Serve immediately. Makes 6 servings.

Honey-Orange Sweet Potatoes

You'll need two oranges to get ½ cup of juice.

1 teaspoon finely shredded orange peel
½ cup orange juice
2 tablespoons soy sauce
1 teaspoon cornstarch
1 teaspoon honey
1 tablespoon cooking oil
1 teaspoon grated gingerroot
2 medium sweet potatoes, peeled, halved lengthwise, and thinly bias sliced (3 cups)
½ cup cashews

● For sauce, stir together orange peel, orange juice, soy sauce, cornstarch, and honey. Set aside.

● Preheat a wok or large skillet over high heat; add cooking oil. (Add more oil as necessary during cooking.) Stir-fry gingerroot in hot oil for 15 seconds. Add sweet potatoes; stir-fry for 4 minutes. Cover and cook about 1 minute more or till sweet potatoes are crisp-tender. Push sweet potatoes from center of the wok or skillet.

● Stir sauce; add to center of the wok or skillet. Cook and stir till thickened and bubbly. Cook and stir for 1 minute more. Stir in sweet potatoes and cashews to coat with sauce. Serve immediately. Makes 4 servings.

Dilled Cauliflower and Pea Pods

We added chopped pimiento to this refreshing stir-fry for a splash of color.
(Pictured on page 76.)

½ of a medium head
   cauliflower, broken into
   flowerets (2 cups)
⅓ cup plain yogurt
1 tablespoon all-purpose flour
¼ cup milk
1½ teaspoons snipped dillweed
   or ½ teaspoon dried
   dillweed, crushed
1 tablespoon cooking oil
2 cups fresh pea pods *or*
   one 6-ounce package
   frozen pea pods, thawed
1 tablespoon chopped
   pimiento
   Fresh dillweed (optional)

● Halve any large cauliflower flowerets. Cook cauliflower, covered, in small amount of boiling salted water for 2 minutes; drain. For sauce, stir together yogurt and flour. Stir in milk and dried dillweed. Set aside.

● Preheat a wok or large skillet over high heat; add cooking oil. (Add more oil as necessary during cooking.) Stir-fry cauliflower in hot oil for 2 minutes. Add pea pods; stir-fry about 3 minutes or till vegetables are crisp-tender. Push vegetables from center of the wok.

● Reduce heat. Add sauce to center of the wok or skillet. Cook and stir till thickened and bubbly. Cook and stir for 1 minute more. Stir in vegetables and chopped pimiento to coat with sauce. Cook and stir for 1 minute. Garnish with fresh dillweed, if desired. Serve immediately. Makes 4 servings.

Preparing fresh pea pods
Pea pods—also known as sugar peas, snow peas, or Chinese peas—are a popular ingredient in Oriental-style stir-fries. Because pea pods are picked and used when the seeds are under-developed, the thin-skinned pods are sweet and crisp for eating.

To prepare fresh pea pods, remove their tips and strings. Just use your fingers to pull off the tip of the pod without breaking the string. Then pull the string down the entire length of the pod. Remove the string from the pod and discard.

Orange-Walnut Cauliflower and Carrots

In testing our recipes containing walnuts or pecans, we found that the color of a dish looked best when the nuts were stirred in at the very end of stir-frying.

3 medium carrots, roll cut
   (1 cup)
⅓ cup orange juice
1 teaspoon cornstarch
1 teaspoon brown sugar
1 tablespoon cooking oil
1½ cups thinly sliced
   cauliflower
¼ cup chopped walnuts

● Cook carrots, covered, in a small amount of boiling salted water for 3½ minutes; drain. For sauce, stir together orange juice, cornstarch, and brown sugar. Set aside.

● Preheat a wok or large skillet over high heat; add cooking oil. (Add more oil as necessary during cooking.) Stir-fry cauliflower in hot oil for 2½ minutes. Add carrots; stir-fry about 2½ minutes or till vegetables are crisp-tender. Push vegetables from center of the wok.

● Stir sauce; add to center of the wok or skillet. Cook and stir till thickened and bubbly. Cook and stir for 1 minute more. Stir in vegetables and walnuts to coat with sauce. Serve immediately. Makes 4 servings.

Oriental Pea Pods

Grated fresh gingerroot will add a distinct aromatic, fresh quality to your stir-fries. If you prefer to use ground ginger in this recipe, use ¼ teaspoon.

⅓ cup cold water
2 tablespoons soy sauce
2 teaspoons cornstarch
1 teaspoon sugar
½ teaspoon grated gingerroot
⅛ teaspoon freshly ground
   pepper
1 tablespoon cooking oil
2 medium carrots, thinly bias
   sliced (1 cup)
1 cup fresh pea pods *or* ½ of a
   6-ounce package frozen
   pea pods, thawed
5 green onions, bias-sliced
   into 1-inch lengths (1 cup)
½ cup sliced fresh mushrooms
1 8-ounce can sliced water
   chestnuts, drained

● For sauce, stir together water, soy sauce, cornstarch, sugar, gingerroot, and pepper. Set aside.

● Preheat a wok or large skillet over high heat; add cooking oil. (Add more oil as necessary during cooking.) Stir-fry carrots in hot oil for 2 minutes. Add pea pods; stir-fry for 30 seconds. Add onions and mushrooms; stir-fry about 1½ minutes or till vegetables are crisp-tender. Stir in water chestnuts. Push vegetables from center of the wok.

● Stir sauce; add to center of the wok or skillet. Cook and stir till thickened and bubbly. Cook and stir for 1 minute more. Stir in the vegetables to coat with the sauce. Serve immediately. Makes 4 servings.

Dilled Cauliflower and Pea Pods
(see recipe, page 74)

Herbed Tomatoes and Cucumbers

When you have a bumper crop of tomatoes and cucumbers, try this savory side dish seasoned with rosemary and basil.

2	**medium cucumbers**
1	**tablespoon cooking oil**
½	**teaspoon dried basil, crushed**
¼	**teaspoon dried rosemary, crushed**
5	**green onions, bias-sliced into 1-inch lengths (1 cup)**
2	**medium tomatoes, cut into thin wedges**

● Halve cucumbers lengthwise; trim off ends and scoop out seeds. Cut cucumbers into ¼-inch slices.

● Preheat a wok or large skillet over high heat; add cooking oil. Stir-fry cucumbers, basil, and rosemary in hot oil for 2½ minutes. Add onions; stir-fry about 1½ minutes or till vegetables are crisp-tender. Gently stir in tomatoes. Cover and cook for 30 seconds. Serve immediately. Makes 4 servings.

Sesame Noodles

After adding the noodles, let them brown by resting periodically on the wok's bottom during stir-frying. Be careful, however, so they don't stick to the bottom!

4	**ounces fine noodles (2 cups)**
1	**teaspoon sesame oil**
1	**tablespoon sesame oil**
1	**tablespoon sesame seed**
4	**green onions, bias sliced (½ cup)**
2½	**ounces fresh mushrooms, sliced (1 cup)**
1	**medium carrot, coarsely shredded (½ cup)**
2	**tablespoons cooking oil**

● Cook noodles according to package directions; drain. Rinse in cold water; drain well. Use a paper towel to pat dry. Toss with the 1 teaspoon sesame oil. Cover and chill thoroughly.

● Preheat a wok or large skillet over high heat; add the 1 tablespoon sesame oil. Stir-fry sesame seed in hot oil for 30 seconds. Add green onions; stir-fry for 30 seconds. Add sliced mushrooms and shredded carrot; stir-fry about 1 minute or till vegetables are crisp-tender.

● Add cooking oil to the wok or skillet. Stir noodles into vegetables. Stir-fry noodle mixture about 9 minutes or till noodles are just beginning to brown. Sprinkle with a little salt, if desired. Serve immediately. Makes 4 to 6 servings.

Index

Index *(continued)*